Dr Brian Roet was in general practice in Melbourne,
Australia, for fifteen years before he came to England in
1980. During this time, he noticed a great deficiency in his
ability to treat the high proportion of patients visiting him
for emotionally related illnesses.

Using techniques such as self-hypnosis and creative
visualisation, he has spent the last nine years in his
London practice learning about the ability of the mind to
create or resolve disease. He believes strongly in the need
to educate people about the role played by their minds in
their emotional or physical ill health.

In the course of his work he has written two books —
Hypnosis — A Gateway to Better Health (Weidenfeld &
Nicholson), and *All in the Mind? — Think Yourself Better*
(Macdonald Optima). This is his third book.

OPTIMA

A SAFER
PLACE TO CRY

DR BRIAN ROET

ILLUSTRATED BY
SHAUN WILLIAMS

An OPTIMA book

First published in 1989 by
Macdonald Optima, a division of
Macdonald & Co. (Publishers) Ltd

A member of Maxwell Pergamon Publishing Corporation plc

British Library Cataloguing in Publication Data

Roet, Brian
    A safer place to cry.
    1. Psychotherapy
    I. Title
    616.89'14

    ISBN 0-356-17603-7

Macdonald & Co. (Publishers) Ltd
66-73 Shoe Lane
London EC4P 4AB

Typeset in Century Schoolbook
by Leaper & Gard Ltd, Bristol

Printed and bound in Great Britain by
The Guernsey Press, Co. Ltd
Guernsey, Channel Islands

CONTENTS

For those amongst us who
have not yet found a safer place to cry

ACKNOWLEDGMENTS

I would like to thank Lorraine not for only supporting me on the tennis court, but also for having the strength to retype numerous chapters repeatedly as new ideas flooded into my mind; Gill for her readiness to convert pages of manuscript into some semblance of order at a moment's notice; my patients who became my literary critics; the tissue manufacturer who supplied me with a lifetime of tissues for my clients' use; and all the tears that flowed to reduce pressure in the lakes of past emotions confined for far too long.

The sharing of hurt is the
beginning of healing

Dr Robert Runcie, during the memorial
service following the Hungerford Massacre

INTRODUCTION

If you know what you do
You can do what you want.

Feldenkrais method of movement therapy

This book is a collection of thoughts about many aspects of
health, feeling well and restoring the balance to a system
called 'myself'. There are a number of divisions to this
system — mind and body, conscious and unconscious, to
try or to be, logic and emotion, physical and psychological,
and many more. Each compartment requires its own
delicate balance to function correctly.

Any active 'machine' has parts causing it to stop or go;
each is essential, one no more important than another. So
it is with the components of the human machine, and it is
necessary to realise when one part is in control, just as a
good driver is aware of when to use the brake or
accelerator. Many problems occur in life when people are
unaware of what component is 'driving' them. This
ignorance or lack of attention reduces available potential,
producing a downward spiral over the course of time.

Restoring the balance to your system will bring you
harmony and energy for you to be the best you possibly
can. To achieve this balance requires time, effort, and an
open mind in order to observe the signposts pointing out
that all is not well, that somewhere an imbalance exists
that needs correction.

Many people who come to see me spontaneously burst
into tears during their first visit. It is as if they have
arrived at a safe place to let go of their burdens — a safer
place to cry than has been previously offered. These tears
appear for no apparent reason and are often accompanied
by comments such as 'I never cry, especially in public. I
don't know what came over me, it was as if the tears

poured out of their own accord. I'm ever so sorry.'

Deep down, for a long time, they have carried thoughts, emotions and memories previously ignored or locked away as too painful to confront. They had found no safe harbour to anchor their ship of sadness and shame. The process of crying and the discussions that follow often lead to calmer waters, an inner peace and understanding — a suitable balance in their lives. In time they gain an awareness that some vital part of themselves needs attention and, as this happens, improvement occurs.

There are many dark threads interwoven in the tapestry of those who are unhappy, in trouble, or failing in their achievements. One main thread which causes problems is an attitude of avoidance; this delays or diverts people away from their goals. Another is a lack of self-worth interwoven with fear of failure, lack of confidence and difficulty in being assertive. Perhaps the most basic is a need to be liked, and this may colour the whole tapestry superimposed upon it. This book is written to help unravel those restrictive threads, to replace them with brighter colours and by so doing improve the quality of the tapestry formed.

ACCEPTERS AND SEEKERS

People can be arbitrarily divided into two groups — the accepters and the seekers. We may be born with these characteristics or they possibly become moulded into our personalities as we grow.

The accepters take life as it comes — 'Get on with things' is their motto. They feel no need to query or analyse why they are what they are. For some, life is a bowl of cherries; for others, the problems are accepted as unchangeable and dealt with as part of life. Accepters would never seek help from a therapist or read a book such as this. They really cannot understand why anyone would go to a 'shrink'. Being completely bewildered by any discussion about the mind, they avoid 'deep and meaningful' talks, even with their spouse.

SCHOPENHAUER? Oh sorry... I thought you said 'SHOPPING HOUR'!
— You see, I like shopping at a certain hour of
the day only! Isn't that strange? I wonder why?
Do you find that?

AT THE DINNER TABLE 'SEEKERS' STEER CONVERSATION
TOWARDS DIFFICULTIES THEY, OR OTHERS, ARE HAVING...

On the other hand 'seekers' are set on a course of learning and change. In a bookshop they will browse in the philosophy and self-help sections; at the dinner table conversation is steered towards difficulties they or others are having. An inbuilt desire guides them to question themselves, to analyse and discover why they are unhappy, missing out and unsuccessful. They know improvement is possible or that something deep down is troubling them. If the answers are not eventually forthcoming, and no improvement occurs in the area where relief is sought, they may seek help professionally. Very often during discussion with the therapist it is discovered that their partner is an accepter who is unable or unwilling to open out enough to allow the relationship to grow. The attitude 'There is nothing wrong with me — if you have a problem go and see a shrink' may well indicate where difficulties lie.

ABOUT THIS BOOK

As you read each chapter, notice requirements (needs) you have and whether they are being fulfilled or not. By this process of discovery you will learn methods of filling these vacant areas with appropriate strengths. For example, you may realise that not spending time for yourself is producing tiredness and irritability; it could be rectified by the commitment to half an hour's relaxation daily. There are many avenues leading to success, but an understanding of the basic principles is the first step towards restoring the balance. Having a helping hand to guide and support may also be required in order to gain the practical experience so essential for change.

It may be interesting for you to note that throughout this book I refer to a process called visualisation — forming pictures in the mind. I am unable to do this myself and am envious of the majority of my patients who can. At times I feel like a blind guide describing the wonderous views I've never seen. Not a case of the blind leading the blind, but the blind leading the sighted.

It is also interesting for me that I have written a book about tears and am unable to shed them myself. The only safe place for me to cry is in the cinema where the tears well up and flood over at the most trivial of situations. I have spent much time and effort attempting to release these tears in appropriate situations, to no avail. My enquiries have led me to believe I was admonished as a child with the dictum 'Boys don't cry' and that this imprint has sealed my tear ducts, except out of sight in the darkness of the make-believe cinema world. You may well ask 'Why should I read a book by someone who cannot practise what he preaches?' A good question, that may only be answered after you have read the book.

1
THE
TRAVELLER'S
GUIDE

> People do the best they can with the choices they
> have available. The role of the guide or helper is to
> increase the number of choices.

What sort of people seek help from a professional
therapist? Who are they and what do they hope to
achieve? How successful are their visits and for how long
do they need to attend? To what desperate depths do they
need to sink before admitting life isn't all it should be,
forcing them to seek relief from a stranger — perhaps like
a submerged swimmer bursting to the surface for air?

The word 'therapist' in itself is terrifying if divided into
its components — the rapist — and most clients find their
initial contact holds similar fears. To face someone you've
never seen in anticipation of baring all — not physically
but psychologically, which is even worse — is daunting to
say the least. The possibility that all the pains, fears and
guilts that have been so carefully concealed for years may
come flooding out is ever apparent as the nervous client
sits on the edge of the waiting room chair in anticipation of
the initial interview.

For many the fears are too great, and the thought of
seeking help is never entertained as they struggle through
the ups and downs of their lives. They choose to fight their
problems their own way — ignore them, drown them in
alcohol or just believe there is no way they can change and
accept their lot for what it is.

Others take a small step and pluck up enough courage

to let someone else make an appointment for them. As the time comes closer to the dreaded confrontation, though, they perhaps think things aren't really that bad, or they just can't go through with it, or it's much too expensive, or some other excuse, and they fail to attend. Often they are too nervous even to ring and cancel.

Then there are those that creep a little closer to the opportunity to face their fears and actually make their way to the therapist, but arrive late, on the wrong day, take the wrong train, or fall ill at the last minute. Some part of them sighs with relief as the conflict is avoided yet again.

People visiting therapists for mind problems which are creating physical symptoms can be regarded as consisting of two parts — one desperately wants help to change, the other is frightened of change. A constant battle takes place between these conflicting parts, and many people seeking help are often actually determined to remain as they are. In my experience those that claim they 'will do anything' to change in fact seem to do the least as the part of them that is frightened of change takes control. On the surface they are suffering a great deal and appear determined to do something about it, but their actions — missed therapy appointments, late arrivals and excuses — state the reverse. Perhaps they are using the consultations to 'prove' they have tried everything and that nothing can be done to help.

A proportion of clients stop after the first visit. This is understandable as there are so many factors involved, both with the client and therapist, and often they do not receive what they anticipated. Many believe that magic will occur and the problems which have been part of their lives for years will dissolve overnight. When it becomes apparent that this is not the case and that hard work and time may be necessary, they lose heart and drift back to their previous situation. This is especially so with 'exotic' therapies like hypnotism, acupuncture and healing, as the belief of the sufferer may well be that a magic wand is at the therapist's disposal. It is much healthier to regard the therapist as a helper, a teacher or a guide rather than as a fixer.

HELP ON THE JOURNEY

For the few that hang on in there, the journey is tough and difficult at times but rewarding in the long run. Having admitted there is a problem, sought help to face it and shared the therapist's knowledge and experience to overcome it, they will notice a transformation, a freedom, a widening of their horizons, which will be beneficial in so many ways. There is a need to be prepared for ups and downs, successes and failures, being open to suggestions from inside and out, and above all to have an attitude of learning towards whatever happens.

It is useful to compare life with a journey. Each of our journeys is unique. We all have our own methods of transport, destinations and challenges. And the therapist may be regarded as a guide sitting by the side of the road; he knows the territory well and offers advice and maps to those seeking help. People come to sit by him and discuss the difficulties they are having with their specific journey. Many have become lost and are seeking help to find their way again; some are searching for a quicker, easier, less painful route; others require maintenance on their vehicles.

The guide's job is to understand the specific needs of those who come to ask the way. He needs to know their abilities, and offers appropriate help in the form of improved maps or technical advice about the vehicle repairs required. It is most important for him to recognise the uniqueness of the traveller's situation and their difficulties with accommodating drastic change. It would be futile to offer advice about a Rolls Royce to someone owning a motorbike; unhelpful to sell a map of a town to someone living on a mountainside; frustrating to suggest a long journey to someone with one leg whose only form of transport is the crutch he leans on.

Very careful consideration is thus necessary to assess

the ability of the client to make use of any advice offered. Often the traveller has a fixed belief in what he requires, even if this is inappropriate, and it needs patience and understanding to help him realise his needs are in a different area.

REQUIREMENTS FOR CHANGE

It is very important between each visit that the client puts into practice some of the advice received. Many fail to have a try at something new, and continue to store unused theory without gaining the confidence and optimism which comes with practice. We can read all the books about riding a bike, but we will only learn from the experience — perhaps the experience of falling off will be the most useful.

A list of requirements for change could be as follows.

- Acknowledgment and acceptance that the problem is yours.
- Taking responsibility for the problem and any proposed change.
- Being flexible and open-minded about the steps necessary to make the required change.
- A commitment to put in the required time and effort.
- A knowledge of what to do and how to do it.
- An understanding of the role you are playing in the creation or maintenance of the problem.
- An attitude of learning from experiences rather than one of success or failure.
- An awareness of your own feelings, attitudes, internal self-talk and restrictions.
- An allowance for time to pass before benefits are noticed.
- A realisation that unless you change the direction you are going, you will end up where you are heading.

THE WRONG THERAPIST?

Many client–therapist relationships just do not work, due to a basic incompatibility between the two. It may be that the client really is unable to change and hence is labelled 'resistant', or it may be the therapist who is resistant to being flexible with his clients.

A frail 75-year-old lady came to see me about a chronic problem of anxiety. In her kindly way she apologised for being a failure with a previous therapist whom she had seen on ten occasions at great expense. She claimed she was a failure as he had told her she was resistant and couldn't be helped. When I asked her what he had done to try and help her she replied:

'He asked me to imagine I was inside a square surrounded by a high brick wall. I had a heavy sledgehammer and had to break down the wall to get out and release my anxiety. I had great difficulty in trying to do this, but each time I went to see him he did the same thing. After ten visits I felt much worse and stopped going'.

I feel very annoyed that this therapist was so rigid in his attitude, that he only had the 'brick wall and hammer' metaphor for every client and it was obviously unsuitable for the frail lady in front of me.

I asked her what she thought might help in the way of a relaxation tape and she described the lovely feeling she had strolling around a garden in her previous house. I made a tape suggesting calmness and relaxation in such a garden in her mind. She made a comment later with a lovely smile, 'The garden in my mind doesn't have any surrounding brick wall, isn't that nice?'

One of the most important facts in successful therapy is the trust, understanding and rapport between guide and seeker, and this can only be judged by the client, depending on how he feels within himself after the first interview. It is necessary for him to assess if his feelings are of hope, optimism and of being understood, or of coldness, misunderstanding and fear.

LEARNING AND RELEARNING

The two parts mentioned earlier — the one that wants to change and the one that is frightened to do so — may be regarded as logic and emotion (see Chapter 8). The logical part is in 'pain' and seeks help, the emotional part feels secure in the 'comfort of discomfort' and cries out 'Better the devil you know than the one you don't', thus applying the brakes to any intended progress.

Learning more about yourself and these two components will allow you to move forward at a suitable pace in the right direction. There are always alternatives and your job is to find ones that are suitable for you and provide an improvement to what you are doing at present.

It may well be that your early learning was satisfactory for you to cope with childhood but inappropriate for adult life. The ridiculous picture of a city banker riding to work on a child's tricycle is not so far from the truth when unconscious forces in adult life are uncovered in therapy.

This learning of new attitudes, techniques and facts enables you to put a different perspective on the problem and build up your own self-confidence and calmness in many diverse areas. It enables a growing expansion of your outlook so that the problem becomes less significant, less time consuming, less worrying. As this process develops, the symptoms become less and energy is used to enjoy external events, situations and relationships rather than being expanded internally on yourself and your difficulties.

This process takes time though, as the new learning (or rather re-learning) is incorporated into your life's structure. The confidence and self-love that develop repair the damage caused by the draining of energy from the original problem. Even if the problem is a physical one — a stomach ulcer, headaches, sleep disturbances — the energy drained is as great as if it is psychological — tension, fears, phobias. In my opinion it is of no value to differentiate illnesses into physical or psychological, the body versus the mind; the pain is the same whether it is labelled imagined or real, neurotic or organic, and removing it by the above techniques is equally successful whether the cause is physical or psychological.

In summary, recognise that the problem is yours and requires your energy to solve it. Any helper, guide or therapist can only assist you in the process of healing; they cannot do it for you. Choosing a suitable person to be your confidant and to share his expertise with you is a most important decision. The pathway you take and the time required depends on your ability to be open and flexible enough to absorb new learning.

If what you are doing is not succeeding try something new; this may not necessarily work but it has a much better chance of success than your previous efforts.

2
A SAFER PLACE TO CRY

I've never been allowed to be myself.

> Daughter suffering from panic attacks who
> was never understood by her strict parents

It may be that even half consciously, we choose our
personalities to maintain a certain saving balance in the
family's little universe.

> Arthur Miller, *Timebends*

BOTTLING IT UP

Our actions and attitudes may be understood on the basis
that we were born as containers to deal with energy. This
energy, like electricity, can pass into us from outside
(parents) or can be created by our thoughts and feelings.
The aim of this special container is to maintain a balance,
an even distribution of energy so that it neither
accumulates nor becomes depleted.

An inherent factor in the process is the need to be
ourselves, even though we may not be aware of this. There
is a real me with attitudes, actions and beliefs, but often,
due to the needs of others — parents, siblings,
schoolmates, society — your ability to be 'purely me' is
greatly diminished. The energy supplied for your needs is
distorted, diverted and compressed into this special
container (the body and mind), unable to be released
unless a suitable environment is present. If there is a

hostile or non-understanding home life when you are a child, a build-up of energy occurs which requires expression and which may cause problems later in life.

The patient in the quote at the start of this chapter had so much stored energy that she blew a fuse and had recurrent panic attacks many times a day. The outlet for her self-expression was blocked in childhood by the powerful forces of fear and guilt. Her energy was pent up like a time bomb, released sporadically in epileptic-type seizures of panic, greatly multiplying her feelings of being mad or bad.

To allow this energy out in a controllable way requires the support of an understanding, caring, non-judgmental listener. Many, many people burst into tears when they recognise that such a person is listening to them, giving them time and attention. These tears have been hidden, stored, unavailable for years and are often not even recognised by the person until they flow down their cheeks.

THE UNCONSCIOUS MIND SEEMS TO RECOGNISE A SUITABLE RECIPIENT TO UNBURDEN THE LOAD....

The unconscious mind seems to recognise a suitable recipient on whom to unburden the load, and the flow of tears amazes the weeper, resulting in comments such as 'How did that happen, I didn't even feel like crying and I never cry in front of anyone. It was as if the tears poured out of their own accord like a spring gushing up from somewhere deep down inside.'

PROBLEMS STORED UP FROM CHILDHOOD

At a 21st birthday party the friend giving the speech produced such a diatribe of abuse and criticism that the birthday boy walked out of his own party. On speaking to the speechmaker later he explained how difficult it was for him to praise; he felt the guests at the party wanted criticism as a sign of closeness and humour.

The straightjacket we put on our children, often in the belief it is built with love, is made in an attempt to help them grow and fit into society. Somehow we feel that if we allow them to be themselves they will fail, be hurt or fall by the wayside, so we enforce our expectations on them, thinking that it is the best thing to do. Our children follow our guidelines either consciously or unconsciously (they have little option), even though there may be apparent control on the surface.

Once these parental values have become inculcated, the battle begins on many levels. Invading indoctrinations take over, and personal values flee into hiding, awaiting their opportunities. It may be many years later that evidence of these conflicts comes to light in various forms. It is as if the gunpowder has been stored and the fuse lit so that only time designates when the detonation will occur. Feelings of sadness, anger or frustration are often repressed or blocked by activities that occupy the mind. But these feelings don't go away; they remain dormant or grow with time, eventually making their presence felt in a variety of ways.

As Arthur Miller so succinctly states in the second

quote, we choose our personalities to keep the family's balance. In order to keep the peace we behave as expected and the build up of unexpressed fears and sadness remain hidden behind the facade, haunting us in later life in the form of physical symptoms, lack of confidence, failures in many areas or just not being in touch with our emotions.

If only we had a safe place to cry throughout our lives, a safe place to be angry, to do our own thing, to be ourselves, our adult strengths would be enormous. The need to be understood is such a powerful need; to have time for yourself, have someone to listen, is such a rare commodity that we resort to paying for it on the psychotherapist's couch. Being accepted by others seems much less common than being judged by them; being praised is a rarity indeed.

TEARS EXPRESS EMOTION

Tears represent so many emotions. Most people have been told at some time, in some form, that it is wrong, childish, incorrect to cry.

'Boys don't cry!'
'Don't be a cry-baby.'
'What are you blubbering about now?'

Adults certainly feel very uncomfortable when tears well up, and great pressure is exerted to prevent their release. The embarrassment of red eyes and running mascara is such that only in very safe places is the dam allowed to overflow.

Tears are a natural form of expression, as is laughter. Tears convey a multitude of feelings — happiness, sadness, loneliness, fear, relief, anger, frustration — and as such provide a healthy pathway to the outside world. However, for some strange reason society has designated this expression of emotion to be unsuitable and the feelings are forced to remain underground.

For many people there is an overbrimming lake of tears

just under the surface. Finding a safe person to trust allows Aaron's rod to release a gush of water from inside the rock of prejudice and restrictive attitudes.

The tears seen in the therapist's room are mainly of relief or of sadness for the child inside who had such a hard time. The recognition of this fact allows an opening, a space in which to deal with it, and a release of emotion that has previously been stored in the back of the mind.

Initially when people cried during a consultation I felt I was doing something wrong to upset them. I now realise the tears were not of my creation but rightfully belonged to the client and had been present for many years without an avenue of release. I now encourage people whose eyes film over to let out the tears rather than hold them back. In this way they gain access to their inner selves, the tears forming an important bridge to health and self-knowledge.

Hopefully people will learn to respect tears, either their own or those of close friends, and in doing so will help the process of self-discovery and understanding. As we learn to laugh and cry naturally without fear or guilt, we develop a peace of mind and tranquillity that provides a healthy basis for the rest of our life.

Lachrymatory (tear bottle) — A small glass vial thought to be treasured in Roman times for the collection of tears.

3
SENSITIVITY — THE FRAMEWORK OF RELATIONSHIPS

Sensitivity is a two-way mirror involving both the viewer and the viewed.

We all have the ability to mould our senses into a compound labelled sensitivity, which binds and strengthens the interaction with others. In contrast, whenever failure in a relationship occurs, insensitivity is often lurking in the background, causing hurt and misunderstanding.

Being sensitive, open, aware, provides the basis for closer, warmer and more trusting relationships. In fact being sensitive means being aware, having all channels of communication open — not only to the person we are relating to but to our own feelings and reactions as well. In each conversation, in this game we call communication, a myriad of messages — voice, facial expression, intonation and innuendo — are sent in our direction. On the receiving end, we have our feelings, beliefs and reactions which create a reply, setting off a reciprocal shower of responses.

By being deeply involved in our own thoughts and opinions we become unaware of the concerns of those around us; it is as if we are only using one half of the two-way system available and so cannot expect the outcome to be as complete as it could be. Inappropriate actions, looks or comments will distance the people concerned, often leaving perpetual scars in the form of repetitive recollection long after the event.

We all realise when we are in the presence of a sensitive person who listens with an understanding ear, allowing us to know we are being heard. His comments are on our wavelength, encouraging us to venture further out of our shells to enjoy the sharing process with a kindred spirit. In this way we move closer with the experience, feel warmed, rewarded and affirmed by another and grow within ourselves as a result of this nourishment.

On the other hand the insensitive person has the ability to distance himself from his audience. His inability to be aware of the messages he gives and receives causes pain and retraction from those around him. He talks at people rather than to them; he ignores the beliefs of others by enforcing his own; he completely misses the subtle messages warning him he is encroaching on another's territory; he is fixed in attitude, convinced his point of view is correct; he is often accompanied by those playing a subservient role — overruling their own natures in order to be submissive to his opinions.

It may be that insensitive people are completely unaware of their behaviour or they may create distance for their own comfort and lack of confidence, just as a bully uses aggression to cover fear. Very often the outer shell of insensitivity protects an area of poor self-esteem deep inside.

WHAT IS SENSITIVITY?

Is it possible to learn how to become sensitive or is it an ability available to a select few?

The essential ingredients of the art of understanding and being understood can be learnt by anyone prepared to become aware of themselves and their surroundings (see body language, Chapter 14). Essentially we need to look in two directions at the same time — at our own feelings and their need for expression, and at the corresponding reaction in others. By this process we respect ourselves and the attitudes of others at the same time. To do this we 'really' need to hear what is said rather than interpret it through the filter of our own beliefs. By 'staying in our own mind' we make it impossible to 'be where they are'.

'I found it difficult to ask your mother for a lift to work. In fact I was quite nervous at the time.'

'Oh, you don't want to feel like that. She's quite harmless really — her bark is worse than her bite.'

This response illustrates the denial of the first speaker's feelings and advice, a response that is unlikely to be supporting or useful in any way. Indeed, a response is very often not required, an answer not sought, a solution not needed. What is most helpful is an affirmation, a listener, someone to understand the feeling offered. Most times a nod of the head, an arm around the shoulder or a general agreement would have fulfilled the speaker's need.

By putting yourself in the speaker's position you are aligning yourself with him and allowing yourself to feel his feelings; in this way you are in the best position to reply appropriately. In many situations all that is required is time for the person to voice his own opinion and have it received in a non-judgmental way.

There is a sensitive time delay between hearing a piece of information and replying to it. Insecure people are often so engrossed in thinking of a reply to avoid embarrassment that they speak too soon after the other person has finished. This gives the impression (correctly) that they have not heard and digested the information given, creating a distance between the two concerned.

And if the underlying attitude is 'If I were you I would do such and such' it is difficult to have conversation on an equal level.

'I'd really like to see the film *Crocodile Dundee*.'

'Oh, that's no good, you should go to the opera instead — much better for you than all that Australian rubbish.'

This insensitive response implies that the listener knows what is right or wrong and regards himself as cultural adviser to lesser mortals than himself. In doing so he assumes a superior role from the start, trampling upon any beliefs belonging to the speaker.

As a general rule it is useless offering advice telling someone what to do unless you are providing new information.

USING ALL THE SENSES

This explanation of sensitivity must sound very complicated for an everyday component of our lives, occurring as it does hundreds of times daily. In fact it is not that complex, but it does require an attitude of awareness to bring it to consciousness.

To get the message we need our senses — hearing, sight and intuition — to collect the variety of information sent to us. In fact the spoken word is only a minor part of that information compared to the accompanying body language. By being open and unbiased we do not fall into the trap of knowing what people mean before they even speak.

The intonation applied to a word alters the meaning completely. A 'yes' said in a certain way means 'no', and being acute in hearing allows this to be translated correctly.

Touch plays a major role in communication in some societies — a touch that says it all, making the spoken word unnecessary. Unfortunately many western countries lack this method of communication so we attempt to make do with speech. In emotional situations putting an arm around somebody provides a sensitive bridge for sharing feelings, giving a million supporting messages which could never be translated into language.

Many relationships founder when an insensitive person continually hurts the other partner who is too sensitive to express his or her feelings. Initial warmth and closeness cools and then widens with each wound; in spite of the expressed desire to be loving, it becomes impossible for the injured person to bridge the gap. So often after a relationship has ended comments are voiced such as 'I didn't realise you felt that way', 'You completely misunderstood what I meant', 'I wish I had told you how painful your words were but I was too hurt to explain properly' or 'If only you had given me a hug instead of lecturing me about my feelings.'

IMPROVE YOUR SENSITIVITY

Sensitivity and communication will be improved if you express your feelings at the time they occur. By doing so you allow the other person to be aware of the effect of his words and actions, giving him the chance to alter them if he chooses.

A friend of mine who was thinking seriously about his relationship wrote the following to his girlfriend to express his feelings.

'One of my aims is to give love to and accept love from someone with whom I am sharing my life.

'Another aim is to recognise and respect the uniqueness of that person and not try to mould her to my own belief, at the same time being strong enough to express my feelings honestly (be true to myself) in order to encourage discussion that will bond, not separate.

'Sometimes this is a fine line for me to tread and I'm sure to overstep the mark from time to time in order to achieve the correct balance for us both.'

There are many simple exercises you can carry out to improve your sensitivity.

- Ask a friend to tell you something personal and check if your response is appropriate and that you received the message he intended.
- Role-play an insensitive person and discover the listener's feelings.
- Categorise the people you know into sensitive and insensitive groups and note how you react to each.
- Help someone to become aware of your feelings in response to their conversation.
- Find out how easy or difficult it is to express your

feelings with sensitive and insensitive people. Is there
any way you could overcome difficulties in this area?

'Tis said that a relationship feeds
On the sensitivity to each other's needs.

4
THE MAP IS NOT THE TERRITORY

Learning is to discover that something is possible.

Fritz Perls, Gestalt Therapy

If you grew up in London you would devise a map in your mind (or on paper) in order to get to school, work and home. You would use that map as a reference and add to it as you explored different areas. Your friends would have their own individual maps — ways of finding their way about London. Some might use street signs, others traffic lights, still others pubs or restaurants to guide them on their way.

Similarly, we create our own unique internal maps to find our way within relationships, learning to use facial expressions, intonations and body language as well as the spoken word to judge the people we know. Not only do we have these external guidelines but we are also influenced by our internal reactions to these experiences, so it may be said that we have more than one map to direct us.

If at the age of 20 we were to move from London to Peru we would be hopelessly lost if we still used our London map to get around. And we would also get into just as much trouble if we believed that the expressions and attitudes meant the same in Peru as those we understood in London. Different gestures, intonations and attitudes have a language of their own, and by following childhood rules massive miscommunication will occur.

Many problems occur in our life when we use inappropriate maps to guide us. We learn the rules as we grow, but these change dramatically as we go through the different stages of life. It is therefore important to be flexible in order to match the maps, the rules, to the stage we are in.

Apart from using incorrect maps we often mistake the map for the territory. We know that if we feel a certain way about someone, that is the way that it is and there is nothing we can do about it because it is a fact — the truth. We become confused between the map — our belief — and reality. In fact if 100 people commented on the person concerned we would have 100 different opinions, held by individuals who all believe they are correct due to their unique guidelines.

IMPROVING THE MAP

Suzie is frightened, lonely and has no confidence. From her internal map constructed in childhood, using reactions to her father who was a most unpleasant man, she knows her boss is nasty and doesn't like her. When her boss has a certain facial expression it lights up a signpost on her map illuminating her father's similar expression which meant anger, guilt, punishment and pain. This points out to Suzie that her boss doesn't like her and thinks she is incompetent.

The guiding light of her map is so strong it leaves in the dark the information that she has been promoted and given an increase in salary. This form of information does not appear on her map; she has no place for it, so it is ignored.

In any logical discussion she will twist the facts to suit the map rather than altering the pathways and possibilities on the map itself.

To be of the most help, the guidelines we use need to be up to date, flexible and available for our use. It would be no use proposing a new pathway for Suzie — to go and ask the boss how he feels about her — as she does not have the ability to put this into practice; that is, she doesn't possess the required confidence or vehicle to make use of that pathway.

Ways of improving our situation are:

- Be aware that our opinions, feelings and viewpoints may feel like reality, but in fact are not necessarily so.
- Be open to alternative possibilities which may be more helpful as guidelines.
- Create the required resources necessary to make use of any new alternative.

MISGUIDANCE

If in early life we learn by being confronted with repeated stop signs — 'Don't do this', 'You are stupid', 'You mustn't say that' — it is very difficult to be free, creative and open to possibilities. The fear of those red lights — criticism, blame, guilt — is ever present. The territory of freedom becomes less with each restriction marked on the map. Some people are so severely restricted by their map-making parents that they choose another world altogether — the world of make-believe, paranoia, insanity — where they are free to create an environment with their own laws.

Many people are guided (misguided) through early life by confusion; the rules and edicts which form their day-to-day existence are at great variance with either what they observe or their internal belief. The panorama of information they receive from parents, unable to cope with their own lives let alone advise others, is so contradictory that no solid basis for learning is created, no trellis to lean upon is provided as a growing frame. The child's mother says how much she loves him, yet her behaviour contradicts this by her hysterical outbursts and tirades against everything and anything. Father attempts to support, advise and praise, yet does so by criticism, blame and punishment. It is no wonder that such children are cut off from their own emotions and allow the seeds of doubt to grow into the weeds of anxiety, fear and self-depreciation.

windsurfing is like life, son
— always remember to keep a
steady - aargh!....

... PARENTS UNABLE TO
COPE WITH THEIR OWN LIVES, LET
ALONE ADVISE OTHERS ....

Adults who grew up in such circumstances are unaware of their potential and worth and so require others to provide the nourishing support they so desperately need. The overwhelming lack of confidence resulting from such confused early training tends to undermine the majority of their existence, and failure follows failure. With no solid map built for them, the aimless wandering to find themselves takes tortuous and circuitous routes.

The directions we follow need to help us with the external situations we are in — relationships, people's behaviour, appropriate reactions — and our internal abilities and senses. If due to early learning we are unaware of our potential, our confidence, or our emotions, or perhaps we believe we are not allowed to express what we feel, then our maps are lacking in essential information.

Going to Paris for a holiday and possessing a map of that city which does not show the metro will leave us bereft of a main form of transport. We will not have the full ability to enjoy the beauty of the city, and will remain stuck in the traffic, becoming hot and bothered, completely unaware of any alternatives.

Similarly, if we are unaware that we can be assertive, can disagree or can argue with anyone, we are missing out on much of the scenery surrounding our close relationships.

By being our own adviser, educator and supporter it is possible to make additions to our internal map. In this way new choices become available to us, and by putting those into practice — generally on a trial and error basis — we can expand our lifestyle to encompass many of the joys that were previously missing. The techniques involved in this map-making are many and varied and are discussed at length in different chapters of this book.

RULES DISGUISE REALITY

Another way of saying the map is not the territory is to understand that very often rules disguise reality. In order to illustrate this principle further I would like to talk about Fiona, who came to see me some years ago.

Fiona's life was in a mess. A Welsh woman of 38, divorced twice, with a five-year-old daughter, she was directed to see me by a caring friend, Tony, who believed she needed someone to talk to.

When I asked her why she had come, she replied 'Tony made me.'

'But what is your problem?'

'I don't know — he thinks I need help.'

'And do you?'

'No. It's not me that needs help, it's Paul.'

'Who is Paul?'

'He is the one with a problem. He won't decide to marry me and keeps stringing me along. He has done so for four years and he is so cruel to me, he hurts me and makes me feel so bad.'

'Why do you stay with him?'

'Because I know he can change; I can't believe he can really be so cruel because people are just not like that. I really came to see you with the hope you could make him choose to see you and change. It is not right that he should behave to me the way he does and cause me to be so unhappy.'

She then went on to list numerous things that Paul had done to her to cause her unhappiness. The underlying theory was that he shouldn't behave that way and probably it was her fault making him so evil.

On further discussion about a variety of different topics it became apparent that Fiona was abiding by rules which had no relation to the reality she was observing around her. The facts that she was 'painfully' aware of did not fit into the rules that she or someone had created for her. In order to make sense of this nonsense the only conclusion she could arrive at was that it was 'her fault'. This caused an attitude of self-doubt, guilt and lack of confidence which perpetuated the 'game with wrong rules'.

To understand how she had arrived in her mess I learnt about other experiences in her life where people influenced her for their benefit and then dictated a rule to make sense of their behaviour. When she was 14 a man wanted to sleep with her and she refused; he was upset and (in his anger I suppose) gave her a rule which lasted many years.

'You are just a cock-teaser leading men on. You must never do that. If you accept a favour from a man (dinner, etc.) you must repay him by giving him what he wants', or words to that effect. She was still following that rule many years later, so if she accepted dinner from a man she had great difficulty refusing his demands.

'I get that picture of the man telling me not to be a cock-teaser so I just give in' she replied when I suggested perhaps she could follow her own feelings and refuse.

'Life should be fair' was another rule that caused her to contort her attitudes and behaviour to prove herself correct. Life is not fair, as can be seen countless times by reading the daily press. She had difficulty creating a union between rule and reality, and so used the future to bridge the gap. 'It will be fair in the future' or 'In an ideal world it would be fair, so I will contribute to that by being a martyr to another's unfairness.'

An extension of the 'Life should be fair' rule was 'People are not cruel'. Therefore Paul was not really cruel and his behaviour was interpreted as 'If he does these lousy things to me and he is not really cruel it must be me creating them.' And so she was caught in an immense internal conflict, causing her to negate her feelings completely, not allowing them to be felt, let alone expressed, as they did not fit into the rules.

INFLEXIBLE RULES

I find it very interesting to observe how so many people are able to ignore or misinterpret facts so they can stick to the rules that have become inflexible in their minds. Experience seems to play no role in their lifestyle and the majority of conclusions take the form of blame — of themselves, of others or of the world in general.

Inflexible rules obviously play a vital role in creating support, comfort, understanding, excuses for many people. By abiding by the rules there is a feeling of being right, even righteous, in spite of the pain or suffering that may be involved. The fact that rules are the basis of any society or individual makes it so difficult to react against those that have been inflicted on us in childhood.

In fact we have two 'policemen' directing us to obey the laws and regulations — an internal one who uses fear, loneliness and other uncomfortable feelings, and an external one using pseudo logic to force us to comply to the indoctrination we have received. In order to break free from our handcuffs, we need the strengths to overcome or face up to our feelings, question the pseudo logic and replace it with experiential learning.

So for Fiona to begin to extricate herself from her mess she would need to develop an inner strength to recognise the feelings of fear, anger, guilt and loneliness which were acting upon her internally and to compare her external belief that 'life should be fair' or 'Paul is not really cruel' with the evidence she has experienced over the four years of their relationship. If she did this she would be thrown into the dilemma of having to face the alternatives, painful though they may be, of:

- Leaving Paul and being alone, in the hope someone else may come along.
- Running the risk that her daughter (financially supported by Paul) may have to change schools due to financial problems.
- Go back to work and live in poorer surroundings.
- Somehow gain confidence to face up to him and direct him to change by her actions.
- Accept she will have a master/slave relationship with him for as long as she puts up with him.

It is understandable why she 'chooses' to follow her rules and remain in her 'mess': any alternative seems, especially in the short term, worse than where she is now. The only problem is that her present mess is likely to deteriorate with time; the other alternatives, although painful initially, have more hope for personal growth and perhaps happiness in the future.

> The mind is its own place and in itself
> Can make a Heaven of Hell, a Hell of Heaven.

John Milton, *Paradise Lost*

5
UNDERSTANDING THE ART OF LEARNING

I am always ready to learn although I do not always like being taught.

Winston Churchill

After a particularly long and difficult day counselling patients, I began to wonder how it is that some people (often the most unlikely ones) learn and incorporate new ideas much easier than others.

The aim and intention of all those who had sought advice was to alter their behaviour in some way; yet many had great difficulty in getting out of the rut that was preventing them enjoying their lives. The intended solutions or improvements appeared so obvious and easy to achieve, that one could be led to believe some clients were subborn and resistant to the advice offered — unable or unwilling to attempt any change.

Avoiding the temptation to label these people wrong, not trying, bad or mad, I decided to analyse the ingredients of learning (and teaching) in order to shed some light on the apparent randomness with which patients improve. It is possible to glean information by comparing therapeutic learning with other forms of learning encountered in youth — riding a bike or the 12 times table, for example. In doing so we uncover a number of common factors involved in the art of learning.

THE INGREDIENTS OF LEARNING

- **Stage of maturity** — a child of three will have great difficulty in learning the 12 times table. It is necessary for the child to progress at his own pace through the various numbers in order to reach a level where the complexities of multiplying numbers by 12 are mastered. Similarly a maturity of self-awareness may be necessary to overcome daily problems; having a three year old's attitude to emotions (anger, fear or guilt) is likely to cause relationship difficulties which are not improved by repeated change of partners.
- **Attitude** — if we want to learn, and put effort into doing so, the results are far better than saying we need to change but in fact being content with the way we are. Many people reiterate their keenness to learn — 'I'll do anything to improve my situation' — but their actions and behaviour demonstrate a completely different attitude. Having the approach 'What can I learn from this experience?' is more useful than 'I hope I don't fail from trying something new.' With the former attitude even a 'failure' can be a positive learning experience.
- **The need to learn** — if pain and suffering are great one would expect that the desire to change would be increased. Unfortunately this is not borne out in practice, and my belief is that the conscious mind has a real desire for change but the unconscious prevents this due to fear, guilt or some other emotion fixed rigidly in the back of the mind. This illogical force resists any change and brings about frustration to both therapist and patient, leading both in the same direction as the long-term problem itself. To help these chronic situations it is much more useful to understand the unconscious resistance to change than to keep attempting to force improvements by repeated tests, tablets or operations.
- **The effort needed** — it is often necessary to spend time and effort learning how or overcome problems.

Many patients have the attitude 'The doctor will fix it', and expect change to occur to them, as if they are passive recipients. There is an enormous inertia, keeping us as we are, and at times great effort is required to overcome this inertia. Difficulties arise when we do not know how or where to expend this effort, and we continue struggling in the wrong direction. It is similar to pulling and struggling to open a door that is stuck, becoming frustrated, angry and dejected and then noticing the word 'Push' printed on the side of the door.

- **An open mind**— as we grow we develop rules for our security, for our childhood needs. Often they are so rigid and inflexible that new knowledge is unable to update them. If they remain in their original state we are limited and restricted by adhering to them. These rules may be conscious or unconscious, but they prevent new learning or change. Any counselling or advice needs to be tempered with the knowledge that it will be filtered through the tiniest pores to ensure it conforms to the hard and fast rules underlying the patient's identity. We all know people with rigid personalities, dogmatic and dictatorial, unable to hear any other side of an argument but their own. These people find it difficult to change or alter their behaviour, in the belief that they are always right. In contrast, someone with an open mind is able to approach each new situation without pre-judging it and is therefore in a suitable position to take advantage of new information. By having an open mind and flexible attitudes one does not remain static, fixed in ideas or limited in resources as Anatole France so succinctly stated: 'Human beings are forever killing one another over words, whereas if they had only understood what the words were trying to say, they would have embraced one another.'

- **Taking small risks** — overcoming fear and taking a risk, doing something new, is often the step that allows improvements to occur. The underlying fear of what may happen is often a limiting factor preventing people from learning, but not taking a risk may be the biggest risk of all.

- **The right quantity** — the information presented by the teacher needs to be in a small enough quantity to be digested; the learning needs to be at the pace of the learner, not the teacher. Often people become overwhelmed and confused by the amount of advice they recieve, and so remain unchanged.
- **Presentation** — the information needs to be presented in a form that the learner understands. It is no use the teacher knowing he is giving good advice if the client cannot make sense of it in his own way. To comfort someone with something he cannot handle will at best be a waste of time and may well have a deleterious effect. If we want to be heard we must speak in a language the listener can understand and a level at which the listener is capable of operating.
- **Time and timing** — often the incorporation of advice takes time, sometimes even years, before it takes root and grows to fruition. It is also important to offer advice at a time suitable to the listener.
- **Intellectual learning and 'real' learning** — often people understand logically what is being said but block off any transference of that knowledge into actions or attitudes. It is as if they keep it in mind rather than absorb it to become part of them. To learn something requires filtering it through to the emotions, not just keeping it in the logical mind; in this way the new learning is 'owned' — part of the person — not merely understood.
- **Learning is by experience** — however much theory or discussion occurs, the main process of learning is by the actual experiences we have. One action is worth 1,000 words. Many are keen to read, analyse and discuss their problem, but loathe to have a go at actually doing something about it. One can read many books on how to build a boat, but until the trial and error of the actual boat-building occurs the learning is negligible. This is especially so for the myriad of

emotional problems that find their way to the therapist's office. Often people who have made changes state 'I just did it without thinking'; it was the thinking, weighing up pros and cons, anticipating, that was preventing change.

- **Learning what is preventing you learning** will enable you to gain confidence to proceed. By understanding how you are maintaining your problem you will be well on the way to solving it. Comprehending your anxieties, fears, emotions and needs will help you to circumvent them in the process of improvement.
- **Putting the problem into perspective** allows energy to overcome it. Often we are so into our problems that we become surrounded (embalmed) by them. This enclosure limits the resources necessary to get out of the situation. By distancing ourselves from the problem and putting it into perspective we are much freer to deal with it.
- **Support and understanding** is the most important background to any learning process. Because we are going to do something new, we need to know we have an experienced guide to help us along the way. This support acts like a trellis to a rose, allowing it to grow and explore different directions with a solid backing, although it may take a little while until the therapeutic relationship is strong enough to support the explorations required.

THE ART OF THE TEACHER

There are numerous techniques and devices which facilitate learning — tricks of the trade used by teachers to provide a vast variety of tuition. Holding the saddle of the bike until a balance is obtained, and gradually letting go so that the new rider moves on his own, is a metaphor for many types of learning.

The art of the teacher is to provide confidence for the pupil to explore in his own way. He must know when to encourage action and when to accept the *status quo*. He must be where his pupil is in order to understand the fears and limitations that restrict him. He must praise and encourage to allow the full potential of his pupil to be realised.

A child is not a vessel to be filled but a flame to be kindled.

6
INTERNAL ATTITUDES — RESTRICTIVE OR EXPANSIVE?

> Change may require time, effort and understanding to alter rigid structures gathered along the way.

The way we think, feel, behave is dictated by internal (infernal) devices setting out 'the rules' which control our behaviour (see Chapter 4). Being open, flexible, carefree, has a similar number of rules to being critical, defensive and inflexible, but the components are vastly different. It therefore follows that we are able to alter our attitudes by varying the component parts of the systems we are using.

I have in my surgery a strange but accurate timepiece — a 'backwards' clock. It is normal except that the numbers are anti-clockwise and the hands move in an anti-clockwise direction. Thus the position of the hands which would normally register 3 o'clock show 9 o'clock.

A patient came to see me about problems occurring in her life and after a few minutes commented that my clock was telling the wrong time. I requested she look at it again and she repeated her remark as she glanced at her wristwatch. For the next 20 minutes our conversation was a repetition of:

'Your clock is wrong Dr. Roet.'

'Have another look at it and tell me what you notice', followed by a long pause as her confused brain tried to make some sense of a clock that by her eyes told the wrong time.

The interview finished with no more discussion than the above. She left believing I was mad and that she had unnecessarily wasted money discussing the time with a cranky doctor.

I believe her restricted thinking in relation to the clock was also being used in a multitude of other situations in her life and it was no wonder she was experiencing difficulties.

Whenever I go shopping with a friend of mine I note the following mechanisms functioning internally.

- 'I need a new handbag, let's look in this shop' — a stated aim. We browse around the shop until she finds a suitable bag at a reasonable price.
- 'This looks just like what I want and I can afford it too, what luck!' — finding the article and accepting the price. Then comes the next step.
- 'I wonder if I can find a better (cheaper) bag at another shop?' Doubts negate her previous decision with an apparent form of logic. After long deliberation and discussion she replaces the bag and we seek other shops to find the right article. Failing to achieve success she remarks,
- 'I'm sure I should have bought that first bag in the other shop. Let's go back and I'll buy it now' — a realisation that the earlier decision was correct. So we troop back, to find the shop is closed or the bag is no longer available, and so achieve the final step in the mechanism.
- 'Why didn't I buy it when I had it? What a fool I am, why don't I ever learn?'

The above steps are not achieving the desired aim (in this case to purchase a suitable bag): they do achieve the aim of being unhappy, annoyed, frustrated (both of us) and self-depreciating (as well as blaming me for not making her buy the first one). How is it that the above mechanism is repeated day after day, year after year, with minimal learning from experience?

A similar mechanism works in reverse for another friend who is married to a very wealthy man. She is covered in gold and jewels, lives in a large house full of antiques and paintings, and is lonely, depressed and unhappy. The steps in her mechanisms are:

- 'I'm feeling depressed and unhappy today. I'll go and buy something which will make me feel better.'
- She has her chauffeur drive her to Bond Street and strolls up and down looking in the jewellery shop windows. When she sees something she likes she goes into the shop and buys it.
- She puts on the piece of jewellery and is driven to a friend's house for a drink, to show it off and make her jealous.
- She leaves her friend, goes home and slumps in a chair feeling lonely, sad and depressed.

Her internal rules are not directing her to achieve what she is hoping for. She has played by these rules for years; she may even have married her husband following the same belief. She continues on the same pathway as if no other route is available to her.

For most of my life I have followed inappropriate steps relating to eating in restaurants.

- 'I'll eat with friends tonight, have a great time and feel really good at the end of the night.'
- I would join them at the restaurant, have a starter, main course and dessert and lots of wine.
- I'd leave the restaurant feeling overfull and groaning that I'd eaten too much.
- I'd wake up in the morning suffering from the excess of alcohol and bemoan the fact that I'd repeated the same mistake I had always made.
- I'd realise that I'd wasted good food, spent a lot of money and ended up feeling terrible.

After one such night I made a decision that I would change

the pattern, as I'd been doing the same thing night after night for years, with the same painful result. The conclusion I came to was:

- Don't have a starter, or
- Have only two starters and no main course, or
- Assess how I feel before ordering the dessert, and
- Drink wine slowly, like a connoisseur, and savour it.

There were many resistances from my friends and myself to this programme. 'Is that all you're going to eat?' 'Go on, the food is lovely here and we're all having a main course', or 'It won't really matter this time, you don't have to work tomorrow.'

However, it was interesting to note that when I did stick to my new rules and felt good at the end of the meal, the others would say 'I feel so full, I wish I hadn't eaten so much!'

The underlying reasons for our mechanisms are many and varied and can be traced historically to events in our past.

I remember being taken to lunch with a wealthy man in Australia and being a little surprised when we arrived at a very cheap restaurant serving poor food. I was young and brash enough to query his choice of restaurant, and he remarked, 'I went through the Depression 30 years ago and remember not having enough to feed my wife and family and I've been a tight-wad ever since in case it happens again.'

History had indelibly marked its scars on this man's mind, to the extent he could not overcome a message he'd received 30 years before, even though his logical mind knew otherwise.

I am fully aware that I have simplified a very complex subject. In fact the question to ask ourselves is 'Are we achieving what we set out to achieve?' If not, can we alter some of the steps along the way to reach a more favourable outcome?

THE HEAVY HAND OF CONTROL

One element that threads its way through the whole
scenario of our psyche is that relating to control. It is as if
a powerful voice booms at us from the back of the mind
'Don't lose control!' It is this very voice which creates a
major resistance to change.

Of necessity change implies something new, the
unknown, loss of control, and it is the association with fear
and concern that maintains the *status quo*. Very often we
keep our emotions under control, perhaps not even
allowing ourselves to be aware of them in case they lead us
astray.

The difficulty with remaining in control is that we
remain where we are. Even though there are problems
causing us great distress, we prefer them, at some level, to
the fear of losing control (charge). It may well be that
powerful experiences have forged the 'Don't lose control'
motto, but a more appropriate dictum would be 'Nothing
ventured nothing gained.'

Check how control is enmeshed in your own life. Note
how you feel about change and the variety of uncertainties
this entails. Look at the different segments of your life

from a viewpoint of being in control — relationships, family, time, finance, parents, work — and decide whether you are in the position of being controlled, in control or free from either. What effort do you make to remain in control of your own emotions?

People develop a variety of protective devices over many years, so it is no wonder that we are loathe to give them up with no guarantee of safety if we do so. Hence change requires time and trust, experiment and experience, a gradual alteration of control in one form from the past to a more suitable one for the present.

HOW DO I CHANGE?

How do we go about changing so as to achieve or attempt to achieve our aims? Change can occur by bringing to conscious awareness some of the questions that occur at an unconscious level.

- Firstly, do I want to change some area of my life or am I happy how I am, even though others may not like it? This is a most important question as it seems futile to try and change if you don't want to.
- Ask yourself what is your aim in a specific area of your life?
- Are you achieving all or a major part of this aim?
- Is it possible to achieve more than you are already?

After giving these questions some thought, become aware of the steps involved in reaching the position you do and whether it is a recurring theme in your life. List the steps that occur in the form of:

- Internal language — what you tell yourself.
- Internal pictures — of past failures or successes, or future failures or successes.
- Feelings which act as guidelines to encourage or prevent alternatives.
- Observe the list and discover which parts are leading

you away from your aims, or are preventing you from achieving them.

- Delete or alter those steps which are not helpful and replace them with new thoughts, attitudes or commitments.
- Make a decision to put the new steps into practice — an actual experience — even though you may find this difficult or painful. Approach this experience as a learning procedure rather than a success or failure.

By using some of these ideas my friend looking for her handbag may decide to accept the handbag she likes after making sure she can return it if any problems arise. This overcomes the attitude of 'I wonder if I can find one better (cheaper) at another shop', and doesn't tempt her into an unwanted purchase. There may well be underlying pressures from previous experiences to maintain her old pattern and it is likely she will have a period of confusion or doubt with associated negative words from herself or others, but if she can brave that storm she may well find she enjoys the new methods more than the old.

It seems wiser to compare your new actions and results with the old rather than with an ideal. We often do something different and are disappointed because it is not perfect, rather than being pleased as it is an improvement on our previous results. The real learning comes from experience, not theory and discussion. Any new experience is useful, even if unsuccessful, as it allows new information to be added to our store of knowledge. Repeating the old mistakes *ad nauseam* only adds disappointment and disillusion, which is so familiar to us.

It is preferable to have 40 years of experience with an attitude of learning, than one year of experience 40 times with an attitude of safety.

7
DUAL DIRECTIONS — AN UNDERSTANDING OF CONFLICT

Too often our behaviour is dictated by obligations to others; in the process we forget the primary obligation — to be ourselves.

The first church is in the skull and there the Gods face in two directions.

Arthur Miller

CONFLICTS BETWEEN RULES

Johnny was to meet Sue at 8pm at the theatre. He was keen to have her as his girlfriend and excited about the night ahead. He arrived early but as time passed became nervous she might not turn up. At a quarter past eight his anxiety changed to anger — he was missing the show and when she did arrive at 8.30 pm he had a feeling like a volcano inside.

Johnny's external needs — to form a relationship with Sue — were directing him to be calm, understanding and loving. Internally he was saying 'She doesnt' care, she's ruined my night, I'm furious.'

He was being directed by two different and conflicting rules, diametrically opposed, leaving him puzzled how to achieve both his needs:

- Sue to be his girlfriend.
- Resolution of his anger.

The two sets of rules governing our lives are:

- **External** — requirements for work, family, society; rules for achieving, for succeeding materially and in relationships.
- **Internal** — needs for the mind, emotions, the body; requirements for the self, independent of surroundings.

Conflicts occurring between these two cause many problems, often resulting in illness and unhappiness. Both demand fulfilment, so it is necessary to achieve a suitable balance, satisfying each one appropriately. To do so one needs to be aware of the dual directions we are being pulled, acknowledging them and responding in a suitable way.

EXTERNAL GUIDELINES

External guidelines are those of society, of our relationships, of our physical and financial desires — a need to be liked and not be lonely, a craving for success and achievement. They are powerful forces, difficult to ignore or prevent from running our lives.

At an early age we learn the benefits of pleasing others and the problems of not doing so. We are rewarded in many ways for behaving according to external (parental), standards and in doing so diminish our own requirements. The conflict is set up in childhood as to which master to please, and often we are in no position to choose.

INTERNAL GUIDELINES

Internal guidelines are for health, maturity, personal growth, confidence, self-worth, peace of mind — an understanding of all the complexities of body, mind and soul.

Too often we ignore or are unaware of our needs — the internal mechanisms struggling to be heard. We block off desires that don't fit in with the external world, treating ourselves badly in order to respond to others' needs. There are many pressures preventing us knowing ourselves — emotions such as guilt and fear limit inward exploration, while words such as 'selfish', 'weak', deny us the right for time to ourselves. The need to fit in, to try, to achieve, to worry about others forces us away from heeding the inner self.

For example, how often do we eat for social reasons while our body is telling us it is overweight, full, replete? How often do we work long hours when our mind is directing us to rest? How often do we speak and act in complete opposition to our feelings?

I realise it is not suitable to follow our desires completely, but often too great an imbalance exists between our needs and our behaviour. We fear we may upset someone, not be liked, be left out if we express our feelings or desires. By doing so we negate ourselves, fail to nourish internal parts requiring attention for growth.

ACHIEVING A BALANCE

A common denominator amongst people having problems — not coping, unhappy or failing in life — is that there is a lack of self-confidence. This comes about as a result of lack of praise, support, understanding at a vital stage of life, and is maintained by a continual failure to respond to essential needs.

'I can't say that to him, he'll be angry.'
'I must do what they want or they won't like me.'
'It's really selfish to spend time on myself when there is so much to do.'

This denial ignores one of the two sets of rules guiding your life. Giving control to the external guidelines means losing control — relying on someone or something to pull your puppet's strings. In order to be aware of your internal needs ask 'What do I want for myself?' without having external factors as the answer. This may require peace and quiet to allow the searching to occur and the answers to drift into the mind from all the needy parts.

The battle to maintain a suitable balance is waged throughout life, and it is by becoming aware of both sets of needs that we are in the best position to achieve harmony. And it often is a battle, requiring painful and difficult decisions in order to remain in the direction of personal growth and expansion. Pressures from without are so important at the time that it is difficult to put them into perspective. Extremes of imbalance are seen with the spoilt child or adult (internal needs in control) and the shy withdrawn personality whose lack of confidence has resulted from excessive parental criticism and blame (external control).

To achieve harmony between the two directions, the first step is merely to be aware of them — understand the subtle internal needs as well as the obvious external ones. The community is full of people following the pressures of society and relationships, while ignoring deficiencies occurring in their emotional, nutritional or bodily states.

Survival is a very powerful driving force, so it is obvious why we submit to pressures directing us to earn money, achieve status, be liked or succeed. The underlying belief is that these achievements will bring happiness. Unfortunately, without internal satisfaction, the external successes are wasted, just as the seed (however healthy) falling on barren rock, will not flourish.

All too often we believe the answer lies 'out there', but like the iceberg, of which only the tip is visible, the majority of the answer lies within us. All too often external successes are not matched with internal maturity, and as a result aspiring happiness is unobtained.

By building on our internal resources, acknowledging our needs, responding to emotional directions, we will achieve self-confidence, peace of mind, self-worth and acceptance; these go a long way towards resolving the conflict of dual directions. In this way we learn to satisfy the two masters in a balanced proportion and widen our pathway through life from a tightrope to a freeway.

- Excluding external factors from your answers, ask yourself what do I want? What do I need?
- Learn how to appreciate feelings as an understanding of your internal requirements.
- Question what you are doing and the driving forces involved.
- Observe your previous behaviour and its importance in the long run compared to its importance at the time.
- Note how often you deny yourself to satisfy others' needs.
- How often do you feel like a puppet controlled by circumstance?

> If I am not myself, who am I?
> And if not now, when?

8
LOGIC AND EMOTION — PARTNERS OR STRANGERS?

The man who listens to reason is lost: reason enslaves all whose minds are not strong enough to master her.

George Bernard Shaw

The heart has its reasons of which reason knows nothing.

Pascal

In order to make sense of our lives we have external 'detectors' — the senses of sight, hearing, smell, taste and touch — and an internal communications system involving logic and emotion which make sense of our senses. Just as we learn to understand and improve our external senses, so it is vital to do likewise with the internal system.

You can only find truth with logic if you have already found truth without it.

G.K. Chesterton

Logic is not emotional and emotions are not logical. Trying to equate one with the other is like mixing oil and water.

There is a road from the eye to the heart that does
not go through the intellect.

G.K. Chesterton

LOGIC

Logic refers to left brain activity — thinking, analysing,
making 'common sense' of what is happening — and is our
first preference for many situations we encounter. The
logical computer analyses a choice and provides solutions
from its vast bank of commonsense alternatives.

'I wonder what to do about the increase in rent?'

'I don't think we should send Johnny to that school as
the teachers have such a bad record.'

'Now that you put it that way I understand why you are
working late tonight.'

These comments illustrate how thoughts are the carriers of
reason; the thinking process deals with the question and
the mind is the territory where the interaction between
external senses and resulting reaction occurs. Often this
process is improved by increasing the number of facts,
seeing it from different points of view, thinking about it for
a while, etc.

A strange grey distance separates our pale mind still
from the pulsing continent of the heart of man

D.H. Lawrence

EMOTION

Emotions are equally as vital to our well-being and
survival, but are much less understood or appreciated
than their partner logic. This part of the system is situated
not only in the mind but all over the body and uses feelings
as the carriers of information. Just as seeing and hearing
are vastly different external senses, each extremely useful

in its own way, so logic and emotion act in vastly different ways to help us internally.

Feelings constantly bombard us, tugging at our skirts to be noticed, recognised and acted upon. Unfortunately they are too often denied, misinterpreted or ignored, perhaps because it may be inconvenient or unsociable to respond to their demands, and we give way to the senior partner logic.

'I mustn't say what I feel or there will be real trouble.'

'I can't get angry at him or he'll leave me.'

Bodily sensations (feelings) come in all shapes and sizes. 'I feel tired, happy, sad, angry' are all represented by a sensation associated with those emotions. It may be a knot in the stomach, tightness in the chest or a warm sensation in the head which let's us know how we 'feel'. Time and experience may have distorted the communication so that our interpretation of the 'feeling' does not coincide with the emotion intended.

A common example of this is hunger. Many people eat as a result of a hollow feeling in their stomach, interpreted as hunger. However the feeling was perhaps telling them they were bored, fed-up, lonely or tense, but as these were too difficult to deal with, the label 'hunger' was attached and inappropriate action taken. So the resulting overweight is added to the initial problem, causing a continuation of the merry-go-round of anguish.

Emotions often interfere with and distort reason, especially if they are raw and tender from previous experiences. When this happens reason is pushed aside, in spite of all the evidence offered in its favour.

WHICH IS IN CONTROL?

Dave, a caring and considerate boss, is trying to advise his secretary Sue about the mistakes she is making. Every time he points out an error, offering to help correct it, she flies off the handle and rushes to the ladies' toilet in tears. Dave is mystified.

He is unaware she is going through a painful divorce from an overpowering husband who continually pointed out her incompetence as a housewife. Her emotions are so sensitive that the normal logic she shows in her office work is completely blocked out.

Some points to help with using your internal systems to the best advantage are:

- Learn about both your logical and emotional abilities and be constantly aware which system is in control, in which situation and how effective it is.
- Learn to balance and blend the two so the strengths of both are brought into play when necessary.
- Ensure the appropriate component is in use for a suitable question or problem. Don't allow your emotions to control you in a clear thinking area, and vice versa.
- Acknowledge, accept and correctly translate the bodily sensations representing your feelings.
- Be cautious about being led astray by emotions that are highly sensitive, distorting logic in a deceiving manner. Try and incorporate some thinking to restore the balance.

DON'T ALLOW YOUR EMOTIONS TO CONTROL YOU IN A CLEAR THINKING AREA AND VICE VERSA....

- Remember, logic is not emotional and emotions are not logical — trying to make them so may well result in confusion.
- Often when heightened emotions take over, as in panic attacks or temper tantrums, reason is blocked off, unable to help. Similarly when reason is master there may well be a fear of 'losing control' to emotion; this fear maintains a rigid attitude, unmoved by powerful feelings locked away by a voice demanding 'Don't let go or your emotions will run wild, and then where will you be?'

EXTREMES

Extreme caricatures are:

- The 'cold-fish' businessman whose heightened intelligence is directed towards making money and whose greatest fear is losing control. This need to control is directed both externally towards others and internally towards his emotions. His failure to acknowledge these blocked emotions may well lead to physical problems.
- The eyelid-fluttering social butterfly whose emotions and attention-seeking devices defy logic. She avoids any intellectual interaction, knowing her strengths lie elsewhere. Her capacity to deal with the mundaneness of life leaves much to be desired.

Many people are brought up in a house charged with feeling. The walls constantly ring with shouting, laughter and arguments. The more noise the more the family realise all is well. I call these people the screamers, as emotion is their main strength and silence represents disaster, problems, loss of love.

On the other hand, some people live in a house where noise means something is wrong. An argument or raised voices point to disaster, divorce or departure. When all is quiet they know peace and goodwill reign supreme. I call these the silent ones.

Massive problems arise when a screamer marries a silent one. When the screamer voices her opinion and seeks a 'good healthy argument' the silent one retires in fear and trepidation. He 'knows' all is not well from his early experience, and believes his wife is angry, irrational or upset. When the house returns to the peace and calm he loves he breathes a sigh of relief, while she becomes anxious and upset as she 'knows' something is 'terribly wrong'. This miscommunication seesaws through a variety of courses over the years, causing a widening gap between the two, in spite of their best intentions.

People who understand and have access to both thoughts and feelings, respecting them and realising when they are appropriate, have the balance to blend these two great powers in suitable proportions, getting the best from life, both for themselves and their partners.

Intellect is to emotion as our clothes are to our bodies; we could not very well have civilised life without clothes, but we would be in a poor way if we only had clothes without bodies.

A.N. Whitehead, *Dialogues*

9
THE DEEP REDNESS OF REPRESSED ANGER

He whose face is inflamed with anger shows that the evil spirit burns within him.

The Zohar, 13th century

Just as tears symbolising sadness, frustration, shame or loneliness need expression and release, so do many other emotions. Anger is one such feeling, often requiring a great deal of understanding to be incorporated as healthy behaviour.

We all know those who unnecessarily lose their temper, screaming and shouting, breaking things and slamming doors for the least conceivable reason. Their anger is out of control and inappropriate, causing harm in so many places — work, relationships, creativity, etc. These people are not only out of touch with their anger but overwhelmed by it — dynamite exploding every time a spark occurs.

Many people (including myself) are at the opposite end of the spectrum. They are either unaware of their anger or frightened of its repercussions. This situation occurs from many different reasons: it may be that anger was expressed in childhood with dire consequences; it may be that anger was not allowed in the family, and seen as bad or mad. For the sake of survival and to keep the peace the feeling of anger was driven deep underground as a dangerous weapon, just as nuclear waste is buried in concrete containers far from the earth's surface.

SUPPRESSED ANGER

When anger is suppressed it has no outlet to the surface, no avenue of expression. Our logical minds create excuses rather than reasons for our behaviour — 'I really don't feel angry', 'It's not suitable to express my opinion, I may hurt someone', 'It's not worth the bother of upsetting people.' But in each case the feeling is there, and unless expressed it will cause damage to other bodily systems.

Recent work in the States, using hypnosis to understand the mind's effects on our health, has shown that the immune system — the body's defences against disease and infection — is greatly affected when we do not allow expression or recognition of our feelings. Blocked emotional energy moves into the immune system, reducing its efficiency and increasing the chances of succumbing to infections or even to diseases such as cancer.

The main reason we deny anger is that, as a child, survival depended upon being liked. Any outburst that caused disapproval created a fear of abandonment, and anger certainly doesn't endear us to our parents. The child's mind reasons that 'If I'm angry Mummy will not like me and may leave me, then what will I do? I had better hide this anger so she will not see it and then I'll be all right.'

In many cases, over the years, a massive amount of energy is wasted in ensuring that there is no leakage of this red poison into the system or out into the atmosphere to pollute others. This loss of energy has had serious repercussions in many areas of life, causing tiredness, loss of creativity, depression or unhappiness. Often the anger has been turned inward, so that people blame themselves for being 'too weak' to speak their mind.

Each incident adds to the stockpile, and the pathway for deposits becomes wider, whilst the avenue for release narrows with each punishment or criticism. A tape recording in the mind repeats 'I must not be angry. It is bad, wrong, and people won't like me. I must hide my anger from everyone, including myself in order to be accepted.' With time the hidden emotion builds up like a pressure cooker, and occasionally (or often) explodes in an unexplained and inappropriate way. (A controlled release of such energy is generally seen in therapies such as primal scream therapy.)

RELEASING THE ANGER

In order to get in touch with anger I encourage patients to 'go into the feeling and explore it'. Using a visualisation technique (see Chapter 20), I ask them to picture what the anger would look like if they were inside it. Generally the feeling is situated in the lower chest or abdomen and many memories of occasions when anger has been experienced may come to mind.

The most common description is of a red, tight, burning, intense, painful, frightening emotion. A desire to avoid it, change it or hide from it builds up as the exploration continues; a fear of it causing problems by escaping directs the person to 'keep it in its container'.

Allowing the visualisation to continue often leads to childhood experiences, where frustration and lack of control created intense feelings ranging from annoyance to hatred. As there was no outlet at the time, these emotions were stored in the depths of the mind, safe from conscious interference.

As people learn more about the 'deep red terror', they realise it is no longer necessary to keep it locked up inside. Most of the emotion relates to the past and is now inappropriate and out of date. The attitude towards the anger is childlike and limiting, reducing assertiveness and preventing personal growth and progress. In time it is realised that the world will not collapse if the anger is felt and expressed, and by speaking their mind and accepting the consequences they feel much better.

Sophie is a 50-year-old housewife. She can't say 'No'. Her friends and relatives make heavy demands on her time and patience, while at the same time are also rude and disrespectful, treating her as a doormat. When I asked her why she had so much difficulty being assertive, she replied it was too frightening to answer back.

Over many months of counselling she discovered her fear to be a 'red feeling in the pit of my stomach' that is very frightening. She traced this feeling back to childhood, where dominating parents suppressed her natural emotions. She was locked in her room if she answered back or disagreed with them, and so made a promise to herself that she would never argue or cause trouble.

When she decided she no longer wished to be a doormat we looked at her fear and anger using visualisation. She imagined a childhood scene, with her parents denying her feelings. She altered the memory by picturing herself throwing a plate at her father, causing him to run away. Over the following week she repeatedly watched this 'film' in her mind, gaining strength and amusement in the process. She was delighted to notice a changed attitude towards her friends and family, and found herself able to say 'No' many times, with very rewarding results.

By facing her anger from the past, and providing an imaginary outlet, her confidence grew in the present.

Not everyone has the same problem as Sophie, but we all have devised our own ways to deal with anger, some more successfully than others. Often the problems we have with other people's anger may mirror the internal struggles occurring in the back of our own minds. By learning to recognise, accept and express our emotions, without fear or guilt, we achieve an internal balance helpful in dealing with life much more successfully than avoiding any conflict which may result from them.

Anger is a normal healthy emotion to be felt and

expressed. Allowing it to take over and create dramatic outbursts, or denying its existence, will create problems and limitations. The relief of releasing the pressure cooker in appropriate ways allows an inner peace and calmness — a good feeling of being yourself, with extra energy to enjoy life.

10
RESTORING THE BALANCE

Serendipity — The faculty of making fortunate
discoveries by accident. Coined by Horace Walpole
from the Persian fairytale 'Three Princes of Serendip'
in which the heroes possessed this gift.

New Collins Concise English Dictionary

Any nature lover is aware of the concept of balance and
how essential it is for survival. He observes the seasons —
summer, autumn, winter and spring, each with their own
characteristics — and their blending one into another,
noticing the importance of the fallow period to provide
energy for the growth that follows. The contrasting heat
and cold, sun and rain, all make up the balance of nature.

Eastern philosophy has recognised this balance in
human nature. The Yin and Yang symbolise the
multitude of complementary opposites making up our
attitudes, behaviour and beliefs, counteracting with one
another to create the whole. Studying this balance allows a
great deal to be learned, both about ourselves and about
the society around us, and may well reveal imbalances
requiring attention for health and optimum function.

It is possible to view many problems as being directly
related to a tipping of the scales by one or another
component within us. Just as a gardener realises that too
much water is as deadly to his plants as a lack of it, we can
learn about the needs and requirements of ourselves and
in doing so provide ways and means of maintaining health,
both for the mind and the body. It is as if there is a rule of
nature 'Excess is harmful' — excess meaning movement

to either end of the scale. We all know of the dangerous or deleterious effects of some excessive behaviour — alcoholic intake, smoking, speeding cars, starvation, overwork, etc. But in fact this rule applies in many other ways often not appreciated or understood.

FINDING THE BALANCE

To discover whether or not we are 'in balance' we can study the results, in the same way a gardener checks his plants. If they are wilting, diseased or yielding unpalatable produce, he knows ways to alter their environment and improve the plant. Similarly, if some part of our lives is not being fulfilled it may well be that an imbalance exists and rectifying this will produce a better 'product' in ourselves. Just as it is not possible to develop a gardener's 'green fingers' merely from reading a few pages in a gardener's guide, so I am unable in a few short words to diagnose or advise on the many areas where attention might be required. I can, however, guide you to places where caterpillars may be lurking or deficiencies in the soil may be a source of problems. These points are more fully explained in other chapters of the book.

One way of learning is by asking questions about your own balance and whether the scales are being tipped too far in one direction.

- Do I look after my body, with attention to exercise, food, rest and avoidance of excesses?
- Am I aware of the mind's requirements for time to relax?
- Do I have a suitable knowledge of my logical and emotional components and am I able to create a partnership between them?
- Am I sensitive to my own needs as well as those of others close to me?
- Is there a balance between the 'time for them' and the 'time for me'?

DO I LOOK AFTER MY BODY, WITH ATTENTION TO EXERCISE, FOOD, REST AND AVOIDANCE OF EXCESS.?..

- Do I recognise not only when it is time to act, try and do, but also when it is time to be, wait and accept?
- Is my seriousness balanced with humour, frivolity and laughter?
- Do I have the flexibility to cope with situations requiring both assertiveness and humility?
- Am I able to make use of the opposite attitudes of optimism and doubt?

The creation of a balanced behaviour comes from the many experiences we receive in life. Praise, support, understanding and love in youth provide a wide pathway for us to travel on and to accept the difficulties that beset us. Many people who have not received these precious gifts in childhood live on a tightrope — a precarious balance in which any mishap pushes them down.

Roxanne is a secretary in a large advertising firm. Her upbringing was one of criticism, blame and sadness. Her inner strengths are so diminished she lives her life day by day, relying on external harmony to provide her with her peace of mind. If anything goes wrong in her work, social life or finances she is thrown into doom and gloom.

Her attitude and action state 'It is those out there who are making me unhappy.' As her work is often hectic and involved with people under strain, each day provides her with reasons to be thrown off balance and into despair.

Sometimes a well balanced life can be pushed into disarray by highly emotional events such as a broken romance, divorce, loss of a job or financial problems that are extreme or prolonged. For example, people going through a long and painful divorce will often find their normal flexibility and ability to cope reduced drastically by the tilting of the scales from hope to despair.

A healthy balance of energy is seen when people react appropriately to situations that confront them. If they are upset they cry, when happy they laugh, if angered they express it. These expressions of emotion may well differ from the listener's needs or the need to be liked, but they will maintain an inner harmony, a regulation of the daily to and fro that is continually part of life. This balance of expression related to circumstance and feeling allows people to be in the present, to be aware not only of external values but internal requirements as well. Having the ability to be themselves allows their view of the world to be open and relaxed, like a bamboo bending in the breeze, flexible and receptive to whatever occurs.

HOW CAN IT HELP?

How can we make use of this 'theory of balance'? Firstly, I suppose, by recognising its existence in general, and in particular how it applies to you. By becoming aware of the many opposites involved in your life it is possible to tune in on areas requiring attention, improvement or energy to restore the balance.

It may well be that the problems suffered are some way removed from the site of the imbalance, just as an absence of sound from a stereo may indicate a problem in the turntable distant from where the speakers are situated.

Often the imbalance may have occurred in early life, and attention is needed, as explained in Chapter 19, 'The forgotten child within'. Alternatively it may be related to the present, where some vital ingredient needs replenishing.

Once you are aware of the concept of balance you will notice a multitude of situations where it can be applied, not only to yourself but also to those around you. It may require time and effort to create improvement, but sometimes just a minor adjustment, such as a reconnection of wires in the stereo, will restore harmony, confidence and peace of mind, indicating the scales are once again level and in balance.

It is very interesting to note that serendipity becomes an asset to those in balance. Perhaps the Three Princes of Serendip made their fortunate discoveries by being a well balanced trio rather than just by accident.

11
THE ELUSIVE TOMATO OMELETTE — DEFENCE MECHANISMS

We all create defence mechanisms for our survival. Some however go a long way towards our annihilation.

Whilst giving a day-long symposium about hypnosis, I lunched at a restaurant opposite the lecture building. The restaurant was one of a chain which may be described as 'slightly upmarket' from other similar dining places.

I felt like having an omelette. The menu listed ham, cheese and plain omelettes, but my favourite, tomato, was not mentioned. I noticed tomato appearing on many other dishes and salads, so I called the waitress over and requested a tomato omelette.

'It's not on the menu sir' was the instant reply.

'I know it's not on the menu, but I really love tomato omelettes and wonder could you please ask the chef if he would make one for me.'

'I'll have to speak to the manageress sir.'

The manageress was summoned and some whispering and pointing at me occurred before she came over to my table.

'I believe you have a problem sir. Can I help?'

'Well, it's not really a problem. I just requested a tomato omelette.'

'I'm sorry sir, it's not on the menu so we are unable to provide it.'

'But as the chef is making cheese and ham omelettes it would be no further trouble to use pieces of tomato instead would it?'

'The chef will refuse to do it sir. I'm sorry but it is not possible.' And she walked off.

As I drearily chewed my cheese omelette I tried to make sense of what had happened. Obviously in this restaurant the customer didn't come first; either the chef and manageress were at each other's throats and she was terrified to ask a favour, or she had such a rigid outlook that no flexibility was possible.

Her attitude of following the law to the letter was, I believe, a defence mechanism to prevent problems. Either she or the restaurant felt that rigid rules needed to be set down to avoid difficulties with customers over prices or contents of meals. This immovable outlook prevented inconvenience to the chef and decision making by the staff.

HOW DO WE USE DEFENCES?

After lunch I used my experience as a theme for the afternoon, and a general discussion was held by the participants about defence mechanisms they were using to cope with life. The discussion followed a pathway of asking:

- What are we defending against?
- Why do we need these protective mechanisms?
- Could we benefit from changing them?
- How could we go about doing this?

What was interesting was that we had all developed a list of actions or beliefs to protect us in some way or another. It was also intriguing that many of the devices were very similar, even though the personalities and problems were vastly different.

- I go blank, withdraw, hide and blush.
- A thousand things go around in my mind. I don't know which one to choose, so I shut up and keep quiet.
- I say to myself 'It doesn't matter.'
- I become inflexible and refuse to budge from the position I've stated, even if it becomes ridiculous.
- I tell myself I'm bored and it's of no significance, even though part of me knows that it isn't true.
- I put myself down, saying 'Aren't I stupid.'
- I get aggressive, raise my voice and override the person who differs from me.
- I leave the room and go and read the paper.
- I try and make people laugh. If they are happy I am happy and don't feel the internal sadness and loneliness.
- I laugh in a nervous way. It helps diffuse whatever is troubling me.
- I change the subject and pretend I haven't heard what was said, suggesting a more suitable alternative — that is, a less threatening one.

The illogicality of the tomato omelette situation was followed by stories of numerous other similar examples. One that stuck in my mind is that of the traffic jam, when one is wanting to come through from a side street and no one lets you in. The logic of the situation is that they will not lose any time by letting a car through — but the fact is that many people refuse, and stare ahead as they remain bumper to bumper.

WHY DO WE HAVE DEFENCES?

It appears that we raise the barriers of our defence mechanisms following 'trigger' situations. I suppose some people may have those blockages permanently, but most let down their defences, with someone they trust, and raise them in response to a 'threat or intrusion'. These triggers may be words — someone says something and you are immediately on the defence. It may be the content, loudness, intonation or speed of what is said that causes an associated interpretation (often a misinterpretation) of the trigger phrase.

For example, 'You should clean the gutters' is heard as 'You're a lazy sod, why don't you do something around the house for a change,' and the defence shutters are brought down immediately with the retort 'Stop nagging will you! Who earns the money to have bloody gutters anyway. I'm tired, I've been working all day, leave me in peace will you!' The phrase and the way it is said touches a sore spot, lighting a fuse, with the explosion following.

Often the words themselves are not heard, but the tone of voice triggers off the memory of criticism from childhood. When your dad or mum said 'You should . . .' it was invariably a criticism in one form or other, disapproval, a putting down. The child takes it as a disapproval of himself, not of his action, and a powerful negative feeling results. Many years later the phrase 'You should clean the gutters' is interpreted as 'I don't love you, you are no good.' It is most important that comments about actions are not mistaken for comments about the person.

Defence mechanisms may well have served a useful function in the past, but their reflex use in our present-day lives is often limiting rather than protecting. Examining how your defence mechanisms spring into action to prevent pain will allow you to note any associated limitations caused by these devices.

By being aware of the way you react — aggressively, rigidly, calmly — you will be in a much better position to let down the barriers of your defences and face the world in an open and flexible way.

I am the shadow my words cast.

Octavio Paz, Mexican poet

12
HABIT — THE REPETITIVE PATTERN

The chains of habit are too weak to be felt until they are too strong to be broken.

Dr Samuel Johnson

Many people suffering from long-term problems claim their problem is maintained 'due to habit'.

- 'My nail biting is just a habit. I can't stop.'
- 'I've got into the habit of scratching at night and I can't control it.'
- 'I'd love to lose weight but eating chocolates has become such an ingrained habit it is part of me.'
- 'I know I should stop smoking; it is such a filthy habit.'

This continual response 'It's a habit' directed me to try and understand the 'habit mechanism' more thoroughly. I began to ask myself (and my patients) what was meant by a habit being in control. How did it start? Is it conscious or unconscious? Does willpower play a role in overcoming habits?

If we say something is a 'bad habit' we are admitting we are not responsible for it, it is out of our control — a reflex action and therefore difficult to change. There appear to be two components to a habit — conscious and unconscious, voluntary and involuntary — and in order to alter a habit we need to increase the conscious component.

The initial action was most likely of benefit — it met some need — and was therefore consciously repeated. With time, the situation which required this action may well have passed, but the repetitive actions had become unconscious and so were not stopped.

For an example of this mechanism let us examine a simple habit — thumb sucking — and follow its progress. A child discovers the pleasure of thumb sucking at an early age whilst exploring its body; studying the fingers, moving them, touching things and then popping them into the mouth is a natural course of events. The pleasure of sucking starts at birth and thumbs, nipples, teats all provide satisfaction to the infant.

As time goes by the security of sucking something soft and warm and finger-like gives pleasant feelings and is repeated as needed. Perhaps the thumb is the most convenient, the most ideal object for sucking. The child grows older and although thumb sucking becomes more prominent at times of loneliness, insecurity, tiredness, gradually the need to suck a thumb diminishes as other outlets for security, etc., are mobilised. Parent's requests to stop the thumb sucking may be effective or may prolong the situation, but in time, varying from child to child, conscious control over thumb sucking replaces the unconscious reflex act, and by the time teenage is reached most children have abandoned the habit altogether.

So we see a cycle of:

- Originating by fulfilling a need.
- Continuing as a habit.
- Gradual conscious control and cessation of the habit.

Most habits can be fitted into this pattern. In order to stop an unwanted habit we therefore need to understand:

- Why and how it is being maintained.
- How to exert more conscious control.

HOW ARE HABITS MAINTAINED?

I believe habits are maintained by:

- The very attempts aimed at stopping them.

THE BENEFIT OF A HABIT
MAY BE LONG OUT OF DATE...

This may sound illogical, but very often the actions and words aimed at stopping the habit actually heighten the desire to continue. It is as if a self-command to stop triggers off the opposite response in the emotional compartment of the mind, increasing the desire. How often have we said to ourselves 'I mustn't have another chocolate, it's bad for me', only to be engulfed by an irresistible desire to have the chocolate. Adam and Eve knew all about the heightened temptation of the order 'You must not'. Or ask any nail biter how overwhelmingly tempting that nail becomes once he has told himself he must not bite it. The habit merry-go-round is propelled by the command to stop it.

- A continued benefit or believed benefit resulting from the action concerned.

The benefit may be long out of date, although there may be elements which are still useful if the habit continues.

'Why do you eat so much when you are so overweight?'
'It's just a habit.'
'What does eating obtain for you?'
'I do it when I'm fed up.'
'Does it help?'
'No. In fact it makes things worse.

On the surface, then, it seems as if any benefit which may have resulted from excess eating is long since gone. But on further questioning it may become apparent that being fat is an attempt to deal with shyness, anger, lack of confidence, or a number of other emotional needs that are not being met by other methods. Often these benefits are tied into a relationship; they provide areas in which to assuage irritation and annoyance, anger, self-punishment and security. Understanding these benefits or assumed benefits is of utmost importance in stopping the habit.

With smoking and drugs the habit is reinforced by the physical dependence involved in the chemicals concerned. The initial benefit of smoking — of 'being grown up, one of the boys' — is long since lost and the enforced pattern becomes an entrenched routine. Many associated situations become coupled to the reflex action and every smoker knows times when he finds a cigarette in his mouth without being aware of how it got there — 'When I use the telephone'. 'When I go to a party', 'When I'm introduced to someone', 'With a cup of coffee', 'Immediately after dinner'.

HOW DO WE GO ABOUT STOPPING A HABIT?

- Firstly, it is important to want to stop. Attempting to change because someone else has requested it is seldom effective. The motivation needs to be strong and the benefits of stopping great enough to overcome difficulties encountered in the process.
- Secondly, by bringing all the aspects of the habit to consciousness, different avenues of pressure can be brought to bear on the actions concerned.
- Thirdly, developing techniques to alter the pattern of the habit and replacing it with more beneficial actions brings about lasting change.

This all sounds very simple, but those of us who have gone through the turmoils of 'kicking a habit' know that this is not so. We may be full of good intentions, commitments and promises, but they only last for a certain length of time. Again and again hopes are raised and lost, as if we are fighting an unseen powerful enemy and the more we try the less success we have.

The initial desire, motivation and commitment to stop therefore needs to be very strong. Most people have been on half-hearted diets numerous times, or are always starting 'tomorrow'. Having the intense desire to change 'at all costs' is the most important factor for a successful outcome.

Bringing the habit to conscious recognition may be done in a multitude of ways.

- Signs posted around the house, to jog the memory about alternative ways of doing things, to point out the harmful effects of the habit, or to make helpful suggestions. To curb over-eating, you might stick signs on the fridge door with slogans such as 'You don't need it now, wait until later', 'Your body doesn't need to carry any more fat today', or 'If you want to be slim and beautiful close the door'. There is even an American gadget attached to the fridge door which, when opened, lets out a stream of abuse demanding the door be closed.
- Having physical reminders of the habit. For example, unpalatable substances painted on the nails or thumbs wakes the conscious mind up to the nailbiting or thumb sucking. To stop bedwetting an alarm can ring when the bed is wet. You can get a cigarette lighter that makes a noise when it is used, to remind the smoker of what he is doing. Or a friend could be asked to remind you of what you are doing.

(This last comment is interesting as often habits are maintained by the irritation caused by partners' or friends' attempted help. They are viewed as nagging or not understanding and so create friction, increasing the desire for the habit.)

- Using techniques such as hypnosis to communicate

with the unconscious and alter the messages which are being recycled and which continue the habit. Hypnosis has proved a useful adjunct in dealing with repetitive problems which are outside conscious control, and a multitude of techniques can be used in the trance state to provide a basis for change.

- Analysing methods used to try and stop the habit, and recognising if they are actually perpetuating it. The internal command 'I must stop' is often counter-productive, and alternative wording may be much more effective.

- Taking responsibility for the habit, realising you can change and that by making a definite commitment to change (whatever the difficulty) you are well on the way to achieving it.

- Reducing stress by relaxation techniques is very effective in overcoming habits. Often the habit is an attempt to deal with anxiety or tension, and by providing alternative means for this the habit becomes obsolete. Also the continued concern about the habit increases tension and relaxation is beneficial in diluting this frustration.

VISUALISATION TECHNIQUES

An exciting, simple and humorous way of overcoming habits such as nail biting uses the visualisation technique described in Chapter 20.

Sitting comfortably, with your eyes closed, imagine yourself as a child before the habit (say nail biting) began. Imagine yourself at three different ages — say, four, five, and six. Explain to these three children that you have developed a nail biting habit and require their help to stop it. Ask them if they will let you know when your fingers go into your mouth. They should choose methods that are fun, making you aware of what you are doing consciously. You then allow them to choose ways to let you know, making certain that these will actually interrupt your habit.

For example, a 40-year-old man, very upset by his ugly nails resulting from nail biting, contacted the five, six and seven year olds in his mind. They stopped his nail biting by screaming in his ear, giving him a funny taste in his mouth and a strange feeling in his eyes whenever he put his hand to his mouth to nail bite.

With another man the young people inside twisted his tongue, put silver paper on his fillings and made his jaws ache as soon as he went to bite his nails.

With each of these two people the habit which had been present for many years stopped instantaneously.

OTHER TECHNIQUES

As a schoolboy of 12 I was puzzled by black marks which constantly appeared on the backs of my fingernails. In the bath at night I would ponder over how the stains occurred. I thought earnestly about my daily events and could not fathom where, when or how they had got there.

For days and weeks I tried to understand this strange phenomenon and wondered if it was some rare illness. The marks came off with vigorous scrubbing, but would re-appear as if by magic by bathtime the next day.

One night I made a conscious and firm decision that the next day I would be on the alert the whole day, in true Sherlock Holmes' style, to discover the mysterious fingernail painter. It was an effort, but I made sure every minute was accounted for. Then at 11 o'clock in the morning I discovered the reason — so simple my dear Watson. As I walked along the corridor to my classroom I would rub my hand along the ribbed wood of the wall to make a noise and a pleasant feeling. This wood had black stains on it and was the mysterious black painter. By bringing my habit to consciousness I could then stop it if I wished and enjoy bathtime without a scrubbing brush.

A friend of mine took three spoons of sugar in his tea
and coffee. There were constant complaints about the
mass of sugar left in the cup, but he enjoyed it and was
not inclined to stop. He knew of the harmful effects of
sugar, but any logic applied only seemed to make him
more stubborn about his sweet tooth.

I was therefore quite surprised one day when I was
pouring coffee for him and remarked 'The usual three
spoons?' to hear his reply. 'No, I don't take sugar any
more.' On enquiring as to why and how he had stopped,
he commented that he had visited an alternative centre
for the treatment of cancer and been told about the diet
that was required to help cancer patients. It was a very
strict diet with no meat, sugar, coffee, alcohol, etc.

He left the centre with his mind directed towards his
own diet and, having lunch with a friend, remarked he
would like to stop taking so much sugar. The friend
commented that it was easy as long as he realised that
the tea and coffee will taste different — not better or
worse, but different. If he could accept this and not try
and compare the tastes, then it would be no problem.

For the next few days he had no sugar and found the
taste was certainly different, and rather unpleasant, but
after a week he noticed that the coffee and tea tasted
more like coffee and tea. He has enjoyed being without
sugar ever since and feels it is a minor donation to his
body's health.

The steps involved in the latter case were:

- Being aware of the benefits of change.
- Knowing what to do.
- Knowing how to do it.

The cancer centre visit and the intelligent advice from
his friend played a major role in effecting a change he had
been unable or unwilling to achieve for many years.

13
FLOATING THE STONE — REFLECTIONS ON A LONG DAY'S WORK

When mothering is smothering, the child is father to the man.

Many times people come looking for an answer; sometimes I can help find the question; in time, hopefully, the answer will follow.

Many people have great difficulty coping with all or part of their lives. These unfortunate souls continuously wander in search of succour and sustenance. We have all encountered them, and often seek to avoid them or their complaints. I have heard them graphically described as 'emotional vampires', draining the listener of energy and ideas without any improvement to their plight.

Perhaps we all need attention, an input of energy from others, but most of us manage to contain our ravenous appetite. One port of call for these emotional nomads is the therapist's office, arriving there by a variety of pathways — some physical, others psychological. The underlying reason is the need for support, understanding, attention and a boost to self-confidence — in other words a desperate need to be loved.

It may well be that deprivation of love in childhood

initiated the lifetime search in every nook and cranny for that vital ingredient. One major barrier to success is that in the process of seeking love a conclusion is incorrectly reached that they are 'unlovable'. This maintains a painful cycle — 'I desperately need love and attention and will seek it anywhere and everywhere, but as I am unlovable I will never find it.'

Just as a parched explorer in the desert frantically rushes from water hole to water hole with a leaking bucket, the thirst remains, no matter how many gallons are poured into the container. The need for attention can be a bottomless pit blocked off from any advice offered.

The majority of people who seek help are able to make some use of the support or advice received, and continue their journey using their own uplifted energy. When repeated and long-term support fails to achieve any momentum though, the underlying 'negative self-talk' needs to be explored.

THOSE THAT SINK

Those who continue to seek advice without benefit may be compared to the attempted floating of stones. The helper's enthusiasm and understanding produce a temporary rise in the level of the stone, only to see it sink in the days or weeks that follow. You may recognise the underlying emotion in this chapter — frustration due to the loss of energy from repeated attempts at 'floating the stones' of emotional vampires.

To be of help to these emotionally deprived and dependent people requires time, patience, and yet more time and patience, without interference, advice or criticism. Fundamentally, the person has to gain his own support and self-understanding and this needs his effort and determination in the right direction. Generally the attitude is to seek the answer 'out there' but in fact the most rewarding direction is to seek the answer internally in the form of care and confidence from oneself. The role of the guide is gradually and sensitively to help the seeker

find himself and accept what he finds. The barriers
encountered often come in the form of 'Yes, but . . .' from
the seeker. And if the underlying message is 'I'm no good,
it's my fault, no one can help me', any minimal progress
will lead to the possibility of less attention. Such progress
is then blocked by trivial incidents, expressions or words
from others, misread to show criticism or failure. In other
words the mind's internal computer distorts external
messages to fit the negative pattern imprinted in
childhood.

There is an obvious contrast between the desperate
seeking of support and the inability to accept it. Any
mishap is magnified, and results in the request for further
help. At one level they seek a life of their own; at another
the attention received maintains the pathway of a
parasite. As R.D. Laing so succinctly stated:

I do not respect myself,
I cannot respect anyone who respects me,
I can only respect someone who
does *not* respect me.

The internal tape recorder continues to repeat the 'I'm no
good' theme and eventually the listener's patience wears
out and a look of exasperation or a rude comment occurs.
A burst of recognition lights up in the sufferer's soul,
switching on a loudspeaker which cries out 'I knew I was
right, I'm no good, you don't understand and that look
proves it.' And another notch is etched on the gun of
destiny, another helpless victim falls by the wayside, prey
to the vampire's greed for self-destruction.

All the above thoughts and emotions flooded through
my body, drained of energy, at the end of a long and
fruitless day. Patient after patient had come to unburden
their loads on me and I had accepted them, even though
my past experience told me any benefit would be minimal.
All my metaphors, understanding or support had fallen on
deaf ears and, armed with ammunition to create another
failure, they left, questioning my role in their battle.

At these times a therapist feels like Cassandra in Greek mythology. Apollo fell in love with her and showered her with gifts, including the ability to prophesy correctly. When she did not return his love he became furious and nullified her powers so that, although she prophesied successfully, her talents would be wasted as no one would believe her.

As I reflected on the day it became clear that those who visit the therapist's office may be divided into three groups, like the triage of warfare:

- Those who drain help without benefit.
- Those who require much time and effort but may eventually change.
- And those who are almost there, needing minimal support and guidance.

A recognition of which group the person in question fell into would be very beneficial to patient and therapist alike. Factors which indicate these groupings include response to support, ability to listen, effort between visits, flexibility and openness of mind, ease with which despair and failure occur, assessment of self-worth, and ability to take risks.

WHY DO THEY SINK?

Some people are waterlogged corks who float to the surface and survive in the rat-race with temporary and partial support; others plummet to the bottom with any mishap that comes their way. I am not suggesting this is a conscious mechanism or that these people are bad or mad or should be punished or shunned. But I do maintain that they are the result of a system which commenced years earlier.

To look for a cause for the continual 'failure to float' requires investigation of early life. Some say that the embryo in the womb may receive enough trauma to start a lifetime of struggle to reach the surface of self-acceptance.

The tiny living organism in the womb receives 'vibrations' of a negative nature, like blight on the seed of a plant. This lack of feeling triggers off the journey in search of a birthright — a right to be loved and lovable.

Birth is another stage on the journey, during which a myriad of mishaps can force a wide detour on the path ahead. The desire for a boy and delivery of a girl may send waves of anguish from parent to sensitive newborn. Physical problems in the birth — delay, pain, cord around the neck, insensitive nurses, intolerant doctors — can all cause fear, anxiety and guilt, requiring years to correct. One whole branch of therapy focuses on correcting birth trauma to alleviate adult illnesses.

Early dependent life, requiring support and understanding for nourishment, may often be lacking in essential ingredients. Just as dietary deficiencies create physical problems, so it is with emotional deprivation in childhood. Phrases such as 'You are stupid, hopeless, no good' repeated 50 times a day for 10 years, will in later life produce a stone that requires much effort to float.

TEACHING THEM TO FLOAT

The journey to health involves dissolving the many layers of blame, guilt, criticism and fear that hide people from themselves. As there is a great deal of sensitivity, rawness and pain under the cloak of negativity it is essential to be supportive, gentle and patient. One of the main difficulties is that often the listener — the therapist in this case — knows the answers, but supplies them in an indigestible form to the plaintiff. The attitude 'I don't know what you need but am willing to support you while you find it' may well be the most helpful and least tiring.

Chapter 17, Panning for Gold, was written as a result of a long day of frustration. By constructing the chapter I was attempting to provide methods for the sort of people we have been considering to find their own worth, focus on the positive minimal occurrences during the day, aware that many negative happenings may also occur but do not need to be constantly dwelt upon.

I gave the manuscript of this book to a patient to read and from which hopefully to learn. She came back very upset at this particular chapter on floating the stone.

'I'm sure I'm one of them. I'm a hopeless case, I'll never get better', she grumbled.

After a long discussion I asked her to do some visualisation and she saw a gnarled tree in her mind telling her she had no right to be happy and never would be.

I suggested she find a positive counterpart to balance the punishing tree that was ruining her life. She found a stone near the tree and felt better with it. In her mind she used the stone to throw — at people, thoughts, the tree and even me when she was annoyed with me — feeling much better in the process. It only dawned on the two of us at the end of the session that her unconscious had selected to be positive the very object that she had bitterly complained about at the beginning of her visit.

Now and then some of these sad people let go of the past, offload the burden that has been bending them low for too long and notice the sky and the spring. How rewarding it is to see a smile replace furrowed brows, and comments of joy and self-worth issue from the previously 'Yes, but-ing' lips. It is then that I realise all the time and effort, detours and dead ends were worthwhile and that even emotional vampires can become satiated and develop their own independence.

14
BODY LANGUAGE — UNSPOKEN COMMUNICATION

While our mouths speak selectively
Our bodies talk in truths.

Body language is such a hackneyed phrase that it has come to mean anything related to the body or its movement. In fact it is a very intricate and often subtle way of unconscious communication, not only to the observer but also within the sender of the message. It implies unspoken messages continually being radiated outwards, and may be either consciously controlled or outside the awareness of the sender.

HOW DOES IT WORK?

In order to understand the mechanisms involved, imagine someone inside you who has a mind of his own but minimal power of speech. His only way of communication (to you and those around you) is by feelings, movements and alterations of the autonomic nervous system — this controls, for example, blushing, pupil dilation, heart rate, bowels, breathing etc.

This person inside (let's call him the unconscious) has a vast store of knowledge and memory and is unpeturbed by fear, shyness or normal conscious protective mechanisms. His aim is to get his message across using all the abilities at his disposal. He will try and do the best for you, irrespective of your fears and feelings, even if it means going against your conscious desires. His aim is to tell the

84

truth (as he knows it) about you, both to yourself and to others.

The conscious mind may endeavour to act and speak so as not to upset others, or will attempt to prevent ridicule by omitting certain facts or opinions. However, the unconscious will give signals which, to the trained observer, tell so much more than the spoken word. In fact in many situations the spoken word represents only 10 per cent of the message given — the rest is conveyed by body language. But remember, as each person is unique, it is likely their body language will, in general, be specific to them. Hence dictionaries depicting certain movements as having specific meanings may well be inappropriate.

TWO DIFFERENT MESSAGES

Psychologists studying this phenomenon have realised that if the body language and spoken word carry the same meaning (congruous), the message is much clearer than if they differ (incongruous). Many children become perplexed and uneasy by the incongruity of their parents' words and actions.

To complicate matters further, in this unspoken communication the role of the observer is most important. If the observer has a bias or strong personal opinion it will be unlikely that he will be open to the subtleties of the body language message of the sender. He will mistranslate them into his own beliefs, and so miscommunication occurs. The most successful observers are those who are able to note, without bias, what they see, and use that knowledge appropriately.

One fault which is common to observers is 'mind reading'. By that I mean that they interpret body language without verifying if it is correct or not.

Once when I saw a patient to discuss her problem she said 'Why are you so angry with me?' When I commented that I was not angry at all she insisted she knew I was angry by my facial expression. I pondered over her comment for a while, and realised I had been thinking about a traffic jam on the way to work which had irritated me a great deal, making me late.

I discussed this with my patient and was able to put her at ease. Because she voiced her belief the situation was clarified; if she had kept her mind reading to herself, much more discord would have ensued.

BODY LANGUAGE SIGNALS

There are a vast variety of signals available to the unconscious for communication. Some of the physical signals include:

- Mannerisms
- Postures
- Movement
- Lack of reaction or over-reaction
- Pupil change
- Blushing
- Tears
- Clenching the jaws or fists
- Slumped or hunched shoulders
- Breathing pattern
- Position of head
- Arms folded
- Legs crossed

and many others.

I have said that the unconscious does not use the spoken word. In fact it is able to use the voice a great deal — slips of the tongue (Freudian slips), intonation, rapidity of speech, hesitancy, talking too much — and many other minor variations which give impact to the spoken word.

A patient who was taking anti-depressant tablets told me during an interview 'I'm very happy, I've reduced the tablets.'

Her face was not one of happiness though, it was incongruent with the words, so I mentioned this to her. 'You don't look happy. How do you really feel?'

After a few seconds she commented how frightened she was that she could become depressed again if the tablets were lessened. We were then able to discuss both her feelings, her happiness about the reduced tablets and her fear of the depression returning. If I had not asked her about her facial expression her fears would have remained, perhaps causing problems.

PICKING UP THE CUES

All the minimal cues of the unconscious language are there for the observer, and the peripheral vision of most people is very adept at noticing the slightest movement. How often do we briefly look at our wrist to notice the time and have it commented upon by remarks such as 'Do you have to go already' or 'Am I boring you?' The minimal flicker of our eyes in a downward direction has triggered off a response in the other person.

One of the difficulties in translating body language is that often we don't like what we see and tend to ignore it. If someone is saying how pleased they are to see you, but their voice intonation or body posture indicates otherwise, we may ignore this because of the complications resulting from recognising it.

The 'truth' of any message given is much more likely to be conveyed by the body language that the words used. The inner feeling is imparted by the unconscious, whereas the spoken word takes into account external factors such as social pressures and other people's feelings. This is often embarrassingly evident by slips of the tongue that occur at the most inopportune times.

A lady who was overbreathing denied any previous experience which may have caused her anxiety. When asked why she was hyperventilating she intended to reply 'I'm sensitive to having enough air', but in fact replied 'I'm sensitive to having an affair.' She was completely unaware of what she had said, but this unconscious clue led to the cause of her problem.

To get the most from body language:

- Be an open, flexible observer.
- Note your observations without 'labelling them'.
- Be aware if the body language is congruous or incongruous with the spoken word.
- Share your observations with the sender, to clarify that the message given is the one received.
- Recognise that often the sender will be completely unaware of the unconscious messages he is giving.

> The body is an open book to those who know how to translate its language.

15
ABOUT FACE — ALTERING THE AVOIDANCE ATTITUDE

It is often hard to recognise the difference between a reason and an excuse.

She always wanted someone else to make a move for her, as if she did not want to play her own game of life.

D.H. Lawrence, The Virgin and the Gipsy

I began to write this book on the basis it would be about being positive, and its benefits, as compared to being negative. As thoughts and ideas swirled around in my conscious and unconscious, a theme became apparent — facing up to various aspects of external and internal beliefs is much more successful than avoiding them.

FACING UP

It was as if a framework was being formed with each page I was writing and each new patient I saw; a framework that clarified the pitfalls and failures that can occur when avoiding a problem. As is often the case, once a theory begins to emerge it is reinforced by many experiences. 'By chance' a book was lent to me called *The Road Less Travelled* by M. Scott Peck, and in the first few chapters he spoke about similar beliefs to those evolving within me.

One point he made was the importance of 'delayed gratification' as compared to immediate gratification. A child's concept of time is vastly different from that of an adult; he wants things immediately, and waiting is 'impossible', causing tears and tantrums. To suggest a lollipop to a four-year-old and then to state he will only get it later in the day is bound to create problems and unhappiness. The child expects and demands immediate gratification — its world is the here and now; tomorrow is inconceivable, and next month may well be another planet.

In the process of growing up we learn more about future events and how to plan, anticipate and appreciate them. Time slowly takes on a new meaning, and a 'lollipop' later on in the day is quite acceptable — in fact may be enjoyed more than one given immediately. But in some areas of our lives it is very difficult to delay gratification, especially if the gratification is that of reducing pain, either emotional or physical. If something is uncomfortable we do not want to wait to get rid of it, we want it fixed immediately to remove our discomfort. This is a reasonable attitude. No one wants to remain in pain any longer than is necessary. Unfortunately, though, the methods devised by our devious minds for a quick cure often do not succeed.

Having a headache, a stomachache, constipation, etc., is unpleasant. Taking a tablet, a stiff whisky or a holiday may make things better for the present, but in many cases it does not solve the underlying problem. I am in no way inferring that we should analyse and understand everything that is unpleasant for us: I am suggesting that by avoiding the issue that is repeatedly presenting itself we are not doing the best for ourselves. If the painful situation persists or recurs, then continuing to avoid whatever is causing it will paradoxically continue to maintain or worsen the problem — the root cause is not tackled.

An attitude of 'facing up to things' may involve being aware of internal messages, in the form of symptoms, or external conflicts, in the form of relationship difficulties. Often we feel or pretend we are facing up to things by spending time and energy seeking a solution in a certain area, when in fact the 'facing up' needs to be done elsewhere. An example of this occurred when a patient was referred to me with a doctor's letter.

'Mr X has had chest pain for five years. He has had numerous tests, X-rays, ultrasound scans, all revealing no pathology. He has attended numerous physicians in the last five years and all have explained to him that no organic basis can be found for his condition.'

Mr X and his doctors may well believe he is facing up to his chest pain by the time and effort (as well as money) he is expending on finding the cause of his problem and trying to fix it. By visiting reputable doctors and having modern tests he is surely not avoiding the problem?

In fact it turned out that he was looking in the wrong direction. His chest pain was due to muscle tension resulting from stress. At one level his mind was aware of this, but found it too painful to admit and face up to a mental problem. For him, as with many people, a physical illness is much more acceptable than a psychological one. How many thousands of people are prepared to go through extraordinary pain, inconvenience, expense and time wasting to search for what they hope is a physical problem rather than facing up to the emotionally painful one.

AVOIDANCE TECHNIQUES

Often our avoidance techniques start in childhood when we are least qualified to face the painful situations that are presented to us. We are in no position to maintain our feelings, beliefs and attitudes against the all powerful adults, so we choose a pathway of avoidance and ignore them.

I only recently learnt about my avoidance techniques

as I was formulating this chapter. All my life, as far as I can remember, I've never been forceful about my beliefs and requirements. A religious story of Jesus sitting at the bottom end of a table and being asked to move higher, while a self-praising merchant was demoted to the lower end, stayed in my mind when I was young, and I decided to play the role of false humbleness. When people asked my opinion or decision about where we should go or what we should do. I generally decided that my needs were not important, and let others make the choice. Some part of me felt good as a result of this, as if I was big enough to 'go without' — a form of superiority complex I suppose.

An extreme example of this occurred when I was travelling on an overnight train in Italy and we stopped at a station and got out for a drink. As we returned to the train I waited until everyone else was on board so I could get on last — a humble and falsely modest attitude. One gentlemen directed me to go before him, but I resisted, ushering him on first. He looked perplexed and confused as I kept waiting for him, and it was only when I noticed the flag in his hand that I realised he was the guard waiting to signal to the driver that everyone was on board.

Another time this occurred — it still makes me feel embarrassed to write about it — was when I was playing professional football in Australia on a hot summer day. My team's trainer came out on the ground to wipe the players' faces with a towel. When he came to me I stood back and suggested he wipe my opponent's face first. I can still see the look of amazement on both my opponent's and the trainer's face — they stared at me as one would look at someone demented.

As I began to write this chapter I realised that the internal mechanism which directed me to carry out these ridiculous actions (and a million more) is a voice in my ear that says 'It doesn't matter', when in fact a decision needs to be made about my requirements. This voice, of which I had been completely unaware for 47

years, directs me to put down my needs in favour of others, not to express my feelings in case others disagree, to take the path of least resistance, to sit at the bottom of the table to be admired and perhaps to be asked to move up, to avoid the pain that the self-praising merchant must have felt.

This technique of 'It doesn't matter' also helped me avoid making mistakes, in case I chose the wrong restaurant or a lousy film. It also (falsely) led me to believe I would be liked more by allowing others to do what they wanted. This 'need to be liked ' is often an underlying force determining our attitudes and actions. It stems from early childhood, where being liked meant cuddles, attention and love, and not being liked meant the opposite.

So I had many reasons to maintain my 'It doesn't matter' attitude, many apparent benefits, many apparently successful outcomes. What I am coming to realise is that by saying to myself 'It doesn't matter', I am really saying 'I don't matter'. My feelings, thoughts, attitudes don't matter and, by avoiding these, I am not facing up to them or recognising them as worthwhile, as part of me, warts and all.

For some days this realisation circled round in my brain, trying to gain a foothold in my beliefs without causing too much pain or confrontation. One night an associate of mine called to ask if he could come to dinner. My feeling was not one of joy and rapture, as he tended to talk about himself a great deal and be quite irritating, but my inner 'It doesn't matter' voice said 'Yes, I'd love to see you.'

He arrived at 7 pm, and from the moment he came in he talked about himself, his problems, his beliefs, etc., etc. I remember thinking I'd love to have a penny for every time he said 'I'. At 9.30 he was still talking about himself as I went to the kitchen to get coffee. Whilst I was making the coffee I heard my internal voice saying 'This chap really bugs me, he's such a bore, he doesn't listen to anything I say but just talks about himself all the time.' I then heard my little internal (infernal) guide reply 'It doesn't matter, he'll be going in an hour or so.'

This time, though, 'It doesn't matter' had a profoundly different effect. I responded to it as if I'd received an electric shock.

'To hell with it doesn't matter!' I told myself, and stormed back into the lounge, a cup of coffee in each hand. He was in the middle of yet another story about himself when I interrupted in an obviously aggressive tone.

'Do you realise you've not stopped talking about yourself for the last two hours' I blurted out. He slumped back into the couch, his mouth still open from his last word, and I dramatically understood how the description 'deflated' is so appropriate in such a situation.

He weakly gasped out 'You could have been a little more subtle, Brian', and said little else for the rest of the night. I imagine my pent-up emotion, which had been imprisoned by the 'It doesn't matter' jailer, came out like an oil gusher just tapped.

Since then I have become much more aware of my internal avoiding device and (I hope) much more subtle in overpowering it. This learning has enabled me to face the possibilities of confrontation or disagreement and discover in the process that the fears I had held for years were greatly exaggerated.

To check how often you are using avoidance techniques, ask yourself if your needs are being met in the various areas of your life. If they are not, perhaps you are either ignoring them or circumventing any confrontation that may occur if you attend to them.

All too often we choose a pathway that either reduces the pain or causes no trouble, but in many cases the reverse occurs. By being assertive and facing the needs and difficulties that may occur, we generally find ourselves on a healthier path, both for ourselves and for those around us.

The main problem with avoidance attitudes is that they send us round in circles, and in the long run no one benefits. By ignoring our needs, we do not progress personally, even though we say 'it's is for the best'. As a rule expressing our needs, discussing them and owning up to them allows others to know the 'real' me, and relationships are then grounded on a solid basis.

The attempt to avoid legitimate suffering lies at the root of all emotional illness.

M. Scott Peck, *The Road Less Travelled*

16
THE AMAZING BENEFITS OF BEING POSITIVE

Experience is not what happens to you.
It is what you do with what happens to you.

Aldous Huxley

Most of my writing hints at the benefits of being positive,
but on rereading it I noticed that many statements were
phrased in a backhanded manner, such as 'How to be less
negative'. So I thought in this chapter I'd come right out
and be positive about my belief in being positive.

THOUGHTS CREATE ACTIONS

If thoughts create actions, it follows that negative thoughts
will create negative actions and failure. Conversely, a
positive attitude is like a mushroom growing through
concrete, unaware of its slim chance of success, but
continuing to break the cement with its soft skin. Many
people in fact use positive visualisation (pictures in the
mind depicting a successful outcome) to achieve amazing
results — finding car parking spaces in crowded streets,
healing of illness, confidence building performances, etc.
   One way to understand these achievements is by
imagining a 'driver' inside us, following directions by
driving where you tell him. If he hears 'I'm going to fail. It
won't work', he makes sure you do actually achieve that
result. Being enthusiastic and optimistic may well be
difficult for those who are stuck in the quagmire of
repeated failures — the continued admonition to 'look on

the bright side' often has the reverse effect. It is as if their inability to follow that direction creates yet another failure.

However, in my own experience, better results are forthcoming if the aim is to gain from situations, whatever they are. And there are many, more helpful approaches than the 'pull your socks up' approach, all of which encourage people to see the light at the end of the tunnel.

LEARNING FROM OUR EXPERIENCES

For many years I greeted my patients with 'Well, how are you today? Any improvement?'

This was generally met with a tirade of complaints and catastrophes that had occurred since the previous visit. 'I'm no better doctor, in fact it's all gone wrong.' 'I'm much worse than I was.' 'All the things you suggested failed to help and often caused more trouble.'

Understandably I was not in a very optimistic frame of mind to continue the consultation. I endeavoured to analyse what mistakes I had made to create such calamities. It is very interesting that further questioning revealed many positive changes, apparently overlooked or completely ignored. I was bewildered by the contrasting facts:

- The patient complained things were no better — in fact even worse.
- Evidence pointed to many improvements.

I dwelt on this paradox for a long time, eventually arriving at a number of conclusions. One was that people have a fear of expressing success in case this causes a failure. It may also be that those with negative attitudes actually are blind to any positive changes. Thirdly, if gaining attention is the reason for seeking help, continued illness is necessary to achieve that goal.

At long last I devised a greeting aimed at avoiding the pitfalls. I now direct my patients to find out what they can discover about themselves or their problems in the time between visits. My greeting is 'What have you learnt since I saw you last?'

This attitude of learning is vastly different from the success/failure approach, allowing a freedom to journey in many directions without fear of criticism. This enables any event, feeling, calamity to be utilised for future behaviour. By directing oneself to seek knowledge from experience, we begin to understand our role in the circumstances that surround us.

Altering the words we use is also helpful in shaping assertive behaviour. Words (internal or external) are the bricks that build substance from our thoughts. It is interesting that, when I ask how people are, the reply is often 'Not too bad' — negative words to describe a positive response. Such people find it very difficult to use the optimistic words 'I feel good' instead.

ACCEPTANCE

Another useful attitude for creating progress is that of acceptance for the time being. Being able to say to yourself 'I'm unhappy about this situation but I'll accept it for the time being' allows a release of energy for creative thoughts — energy that had previously been used for worry or self-criticism.

An elderly lady with a prolonged history of shortness of breath and depression was continually fighting her difficulties. She bemoaned the fact that she was suffering, and sought remedies far and wide. One night she telephoned a relative to complain, who retorted 'Your illness is not going to change. You'd better learn to accept it and live with it.'

She was flabbergasted by his irate reply and angry at his attitude, but his words sank in and she decided she had better accept her illness and make the best of things. A few days later she was amazed to notice that her depression had lifted considerably and, instead of six times a day, she was only using her inhaler once.

An associated understanding — I'm OK, even if I haven't achieved what I desire' allows you to accept that you are doing the best you can and that perhaps external factors beyond your control are influencing the situation. If you realise you could have behaved otherwise, then using this influence as a learning process guides you in a more creative direction.

LIVING POSITIVELY

Many people spend time and energy ruminating about failures, reinforcing the belief that 'things won't work out'. This mentality of failure relies on the 'What if's' and 'If only's' to prevent progress. In fact it is nearly always possible to glean positive learning from any experience, no matter how hopeless it may seem at the time. One way of doing this is to use the word 'challenge' rather than 'problem' or 'difficulty'; by doing so you are directed towards dealing with a challenge, not being stumped by a problem.

It is necessary to take responsibility and apply this positive attitude towards yourself — your feelings, behaviour and beliefs. Of course it is unreasonable to expect benefits from others, as Woody Allen did when he said 'If only God would give me a clear sign. Like making a large deposit in my name in a Swiss bank.' And it is also unreasonable to diminish your self respect or be your own worst enemy by denigrating your true worth, as Shakespeare said in his first sonnet.

> But thou, contracted to thine own bright eyes,
> Feed'st thy light's flame with self-substantial fuel,
> Making a famine where abundance lies,
> Thyself thy foe to thy sweet self too cruel.

It may often be necessary to have someone else to support and guide you on your road to success. This person has the difficult role of not interfering or advising, but of acting as a mirror to your own thoughts, guiding you away from the

defeatist thoughts. They will be able to point out
alternative views, possible strengths, and add an essential
ingredient — encouragement.

However, by stating to yourself 'I'm going to . . .' you
are taking responsibility. This differs from 'I should . . .' or
'He told me to . . .' or 'It will be difficult to . . .', all of
which imply that some external force is causing the
decision.

A positive attitude is a very powerful force, proven over
and over again in all walks of life. It is the gold at the end
of the rainbow, worth the vast amount of time and energy
that may be necessary to achieve it. In many cases the
ability to be optimistic and hopeful completely changes
people's lives. The journey to discover your real potential
may be in a different direction than you anticipate, but
will take you through such interesting territories that the
adventure will provide a worthwhile experience in itself.

> Seize this very minute;
> What you can do or dream
> you can do, begin it;
> Boldness has genius, power
> and magic to do it.
> Only engage and then the
> mind grows heated;
> Begin and the work will
> be completed.
>
> Goethe

17
PANNING FOR GOLD — HOW TO BUILD SELF-CONFIDENCE

As you go through life make this your goal,
Keep your eye upon the doughnut and not upon the
                                                        hole.
                                        Sign in a doughnut café

If I were to choose the most common underlying failure in all the people who seek help it would be their lack of self-worth. This basic non-belief in oneself is the cause of a multitude of symptoms and problems, representing the spectrum of ailments crossing the doctor's threshold.

This lack of confidence invariably comes from many years of erosion by others, through childhood, teenage and marriage. Instead of support and understanding, constant criticism wears away inner calmness, just as continual dripping of water wears away the stone. Often when others have ceased their blaming accusations, we continue it ourselves with self-criticism and negative comments about ourselves, our achievements, our beliefs.

It is this maintenance of self-disapproval which ensures that our confidence remains at a low ebb, causing a life of unhappiness and failure, just as dampness enables moss to cover the stone. People with low self-esteem seem to attract problems that evade others. They miss out on jobs, money, relationships and enjoyment and are dogged by ill-health and bad luck — it always rains on their holidays, they catch the 'flu when invited to dinner and lose the telephone number of promising job applications.

But how can we change a situation where each day is unfulfilling and hope is minimal?

SELF-CONFIDENCE

The first (and main) step is to replenish the coffers in the overdrawn bank account at the back of the mind. Confidence has been drained by continual withdrawals of criticism, guilt, fear and shame. Memories dating from early life remind us we are no good, a failure, doomed to unhappiness. It is essential to store some positive experiences and restore the balance.

I have called the method I use 'panning for gold'. It means recovering positive daily experiences, and storing them in a ledger as well as the mind. The comparison is with a gold prospector, filling his pan with dirt then sifting it to find the specks of gold in the bottom.

To recognise 'specks of gold', think of how you would like to be — looks, attitude, feelings, actions, relationships, work, etc. Then, anything that happens to you during the day that is on the pathway to this 'future you' is a piece of gold — anything you do, feel, see or receive that fits in with what you want should be entered in a diary.

To build self-confidence, view the past 24 hours just as the prospector views his dirt-filled pan. It is likely there will be much 'dirt' — routine events, minor failures, boredom, etc. — but there is no need to concentrate on it, just as the prospector ignores the dirt swirling around in his pan.

Instead, choose events, experiences, thoughts and feelings which have pleased you and note them in a 'confidence diary' — a book specially set aside for daily entries of 'gold discovered'. Anything, large or small, with which you feel pleased goes into the book, especially learning experiences, risks taken, achievements, difficult expression of feelings, acceptance of yourself, standing up for your beliefs, enjoyment of surroundings, praise from another. There are a multitude of specks of gold available for you to acknowledge and write down.

It is important not to diminish any of these positive events or words by comments such as 'It's only luck, after all', 'They didn't mean what they said', 'I bet it won't happen again'. Be like an actor receiving applause — drink it in, absorb it. It will be restoring your bank balance in yourself, shining light into the darkness, allowing flowers to replace the moss.

In time you will become aware of positive events and possibilities as they arise. You will recognise that you have choices, and begin to choose those actions or words which will result in gold. Focusing your attention in this way will enable you to break the force of habit that results in continual self-criticism, replacing it with self-acceptance and praise.

At the end of each week, as you read your diary, you will be able to warm youself with the comments and achievements contained within it. Then you can set a target for some slight improvement in the following week; add to the work already done, and provide a further step in the direction of success. Learn from your mistakes and ensure you don't repeat them.

Whatever you do, don't focus on your specific problems, whatever they may be; they will diminish as you build up positive attitudes towards yourself. Regard any problems you have as challenges and tackle them as such. A saying, to be engraved in the back (and front) of your mind is 'A problem is only an opportunity in disguise.'

STEPS TO BUILD SELF-CONFIDENCE

- Allow 20 minutes each evening to reflect on the day's events.
- Note positive aspects of the day — things done, thoughts or good feelings.
- Dwell on them as if savouring a delicious morsel of food and write them in your diary. It doesn't matter how small or trivial these specks of gold are.

- During the day become aware of alternatives available to you, and choose the positive ones, the new ones, perhaps the more difficult or risky ones.
- At the end of the week spend time slowly reading the diary, enjoying the positive recollections stored in the pages.
- Make a resolution to try some new things in the next week, to 'enlarge your world', building your self-confidence through experience.
- You may need to push yourself to do things you don't 'feel' like doing in order to expand your limitations. Avoidance is only rarely a successful technique for life.
- Remember that it is always possible to view experiences in a positive light — even if only to learn from them. Have an attitude of 'What can I learn' from whatever troubles you.
- Be adventurous and aware of your 'real' feelings, not advice from others or feelings that have been grafted on to you from the criticism of others.
- Allow time for your store to be replenished. Be patient so that hope becomes a pleasant ingredient in your beliefs.

> Defeat has no space
> In his alphabet.
>
> Lotte Kramer, German poet

18
IN SEARCH OF THE 'REAL ME'

Any life, no matter how long and complex it may be, is made up of a SINGLE MOMENT — the moment in which a man finds out, once and for all, who he is.

Jorge Luis Borges, Argentine writer

To what there is
There is
What there isn't.

In June 1987 two cars collided head on in Seville, Spain. In one car was tall slender Maria Nieves; in the other was pug-nosed plump Maria del Amore who wore corrective braces on her teeth. Both girls in their 20s were severely injured and taken to hospital unconscious.

In the casualty ward their belongings were mixed up, causing the hospital staff to believe Maria Nieves was Maria del Amore and vice versa. Soon after arrival in hospital Maria Nieves died, but Maria del Amore's parents were notified that their daughter had died. The real Maria del Amore, believed to be Maria Nieves, was transferred in a coma to the intensive care ward of another hospital, where she lay unconscious on a life support system. The Nieve's family waited around her bed watching and praying for their daughter to regain consciousness.

After 18 days she came out of the coma and the excitement and joy of the Nieves family blinded them to the changes in appearance their 'daughter' had made since the tragedy. She was taken home to recuperate, her mother sleeping in a bed next to her, looking after her every need.

Maria had no memory of her accident or who she was; the trauma to her brain had given her severe amnesia. There were however some unusual reactions to members of the family, whom she treated as strangers, and her habit of repeating 'Maria Amore' was interpreted as an expression of love for her family. Over a period of time, due to depression and strange behaviour, the family sought help from a therapist to speed up the process of healing. He encouraged her to talk and remember and was somewhat mystified by her comments about places she could not have known. He gave her shock treatment for her severe depression and was increasingly worried about her failure to return to health.

One day she scribbled a strange message on a scrap of paper which caught the eye of the therapist:

to what there is there is what there isn't.

He pondered over this writing for some time and decided it was a plea for help from her unconscious mind. He researched the records at the original hospital and contacted a friend from the village where Maria del Amore lived, asking him to come and see Maria Nieves, in case she was really Maria del Amore. The friend revealed her true identity and the terrible mistake was recognised, allowing Maria to return to her rightful parents.

This strange tangle was unravelled because the 'real Maria' deep inside had the courage and ingenuity to overcome a battered and bewildered mind and send a message to the outside world for help. In spite of the trauma of the accident and the intense disturbance from shock treatment, the 'real person' inside knew 'she was not what she was' and created the cryptic note — like a shipwreck's message in a bottle — to save her very soul from a life of mistaken identity.

THE 'REAL' PERSON INSIDE

A useful concept in understanding our feelings is that of the 'real' person inside us. By focusing on this idea we learn a great deal about our attitudes and actions and the resulting enjoyment from them. We all know how experiences modify our behaviour, creating opportunities for success or failure. Underneath the layers of influence is the 'real you', the genuine article, with its own special sensitivity to the surrounding world.

The closer this central person is to the one observed by others, the more able he is to enjoy his full potential. The less distorted the shadow, the closer it is to the image represented. The philosophy of the inner being is 'I need to be liked', and external behaviour is created to achieve this aim. However, as André Gide, the French writer, stated, 'It is better to be hated for what you are than loved for what you are not.'

Every day of our lives there is pressure to act or react differently from our own desires; more so in childhood, but not reduced with the responsibilities of adulthood. It is extremely difficult to think, act and express feelings as they really are and at the same time maintain harmony in relationship and society.

It is so common to hear denial of the self by phrases such as 'I shouldn't think that way' or 'I'm too weak to say what I need', indicating that the 'real me' is being pushed aside to satisfy external requirements.

WHY DO WE HIDE?

The most likely reason for our behaviour is that 'the real me' is very sensitive, being easily hurt if not protected. Just as a hermit crab chooses a shell to protect its sensitive backside against predators, so we put up barriers to shield our inner personality. These walls are seen as the false personality placed in front to receive challenges from the outside world. The problem with this method of survival is that walls act in two ways, not only keeping

offenders out but also denying freedom to those inside.
Chinese emperors and their courtiers were obliged to live
within the walled confines of the Forbidden City in order
to protect them from the outside hordes. Those protective
walls also ensured that the Emperor was unable to enjoy
the vast number of pleasures China had to offer.

It may well be that our walls are protective devices in
continual fluctuation and change, depending on who or
what is out there. This mechanism allows our inner
sensitive 'real' layers to be exposed only to those we trust
and feel close to, whilst the more peripheral guarded ones
keep people at bay. These outer 'characters' present the
behaviour we wish to be acknowledged by, achieve our
desires for us and protect the 'real me' at the same time.

This role playing, although appearing to be temporarily
successful, in the long run denies the 'real self' exposure to
life, to reality, to interaction with others. In time the
characters created to disguise and protect in fact force
contortions on behaviour and belief, contortions too
difficult to maintain. We live behind our faces, while they
front for us. Only when courage allows the mask to be
discarded can the world respond to the 'real me', creating
peace of mind and harmony in the process.

WHO IS THE 'REAL' ME?

So how do we know who this 'real me' is, this hypothetical
stranger meant to occupy our central core?

The first step along the pathway of discovery is to
accept the concept that such a person really exists. Once
this barrier has been passed the rest of the journey is easy,
a journey involving the removal of layers — cleaning the
grime and cobwebs from an attic window, allowing beams
of sunlight in to help discover the multitude of treasures
stored there.

Awareness is the main vehicle for your travel —
awareness of how the 'real me' behaves, thinks and feels
about challenges, situations and interactions occurring
daily. By being open to yourself you will gradually (or even

suddenly) notice how your behaviour differs from your desires, needs and feelings.

By contacting this mysterious person we build up an internal dialogue. 'What would the real me do now? What do I really feel about this?' This dialogue encourages a recognition and promotion of your basic personality; by having its presence acknowledged and encouraged, the real self can come out of hiding and throw off the dampening layers of opinion and distortion which have hidden it for years.

Some time after your acceptance and recognition of this inner personality you will be surprised to find it speaking out for itself. It may be an action, phrase or unusual reaction that indicates its coming of age. What will be even more rewarding will be the fascinating ripple effect that then occurs in others in response to 'the real you'.

Dorothy suffered from back pain for years. She was married to a dependent husband who allowed her to shoulder all the family responsibilities. It was as if she was carrying him and everything else on her back, and this was causing her the pain.

Amongst her problems was the fact that her husband David never made her a cup of tea. Although this may seem trivial, it irritated Dorothy immensely and no matter how often she asked him, David would delay, forget, make it too weak, too sweet or spill it in the saucer, requiring her to get her own.

We discussed the 'real Dorothy', her wishes and needs in the marriage, and her complaints of always being forced to be in charge. She stated that the real Dorothy would be more assertive and direct David to take responsibility for his share of the family commitments. Over a period of time she managed to achieve this and was relieved to have time to put her feet up occasionally.

One day she remarked to me, 'Why did you telephone David?' I commented that I had not done so, but why did she ask?

'I was sure you must have contacted him, because he has made tea for me every day since the last visit. This is the first time it has ever happened in 30 years of marriage, and he even does it without me asking.'

Her changed attitude had, in some mysterious way, triggered a response in David (the ripple effect), achieving something that 30 years of nagging and irritation had failed to do.

Man who man would be
must rule the empire of himself.

Percy Byshe Shelley

19
THE FORGOTTEN CHILD WITHIN

Whenever a child lies you will always find a severe parent. A lie would have no sense unless the truth were felt to be dangerous.

Alfred Adler, analyst

Children's talent to endure stems from their ignorance of alternatives.
Maya Angelou, *I Know Why The Caged Bird Sings*

The most successful technique I have found to encourage people to gain confidence and let go of harmful restrictions is that of 'helping the unhappy child within'.

Most of our fears were learnt in childhood; they can be viewed as belonging to the child we once were, who is still limiting our behaviour. By using this comparison it is possible to recreate the child in our imagination, spend suitable time with him (or her) and help him realise he no longer needs to cling to his insecurity (or methods used at that time) but can join us in the real world of the adult.

The basis of this exercise is to regard our feelings (or distortion of them) as being a signal from a child requiring attention. By playing this fantasy game and spending time being with the child, great changes will occur, resulting in growth of self-understanding, peace of mind and confidence to deal with existing challenges.

Virginia was a schoolteacher whose life was disturbed by a constant nagging feeling of failure. Whenever she gave a lesson or talked to parents she 'knew' they felt she was incompetent. In order to overcome this she had become a 'workaholic', going over her lessons until 2 am, with resulting tiredness, reinforcing the internal belief that she was not up to standard as a teacher.

This style of living had persisted for five years, with increasing weariness and despair. She confided in a close friend that she was running out of steam and the effort of continuing each day was becoming too much for her. Her friend became worried and directed her to me for help.

During an early interview I explained the principle of 'the forgotten child within' who was struggling to perform to someone else's standards. She nodded in agreement, indicating some part of her recognised the metaphor as being appropriate for her own plight. I asked her to relax and allow her imagination to take over so that a picture of young Virginia could pop into her mind. She imagined herself age seven being criticised by her father for doing badly in a spelling exam. As she described the scene she remembered feeling guilty and unwanted, a feeling she described as heaviness in her chest.

I suggested she move the picture of the seven-year-old Virginia into her chest — the place representing that emotion — and have herself as the adult sitting next to her. After a little while she indicated that had happened.

I then asked her to spend some time helping the little girl to feel better — less guilty and more loved. This required patience, understanding, caring and being non-judgemental. I left her alone for a few minutes as she was intent on this internal process, and noticed some tears fall gently down her cheeks.

'I feel very sorry for the little girl. She feels she is no good and will never be any good. She tries so hard for her Daddy but he never seems pleased with her', she sobbed.

I suggested she explain to the seven year old that she is a normal and healthy little girl; there is nothing wrong with her and in fact she grows up to be a schoolteacher. Perhaps her Daddy is trying to help but doesn't

CHILDREN'S TALENT TO ENDURE STEMS FROM
IGNORANCE OF ALTERNATIVES...

understand her and now you (as an adult) will be with
her from now on as a friend and helper so that things
will get better.

She opened her eyes, brushed the tears away and
remained silent for a few minutes. I explained that her
present doubts and insecurity were related to the little
girl inside who did not receive the support and
encouragement she needed in order to grow and gain
confidence in herself. I asked her to spend time each
day with the little girl, acting as a good parent and
helping her to like herself.

Over a period of weeks Virginia spend half an hour a
day, as well as times travelling to work, communicating
with the 'young girl in her chest'. There were many
occasions of sadness and anger, and other times of
peace and learning. She also made a decision to take
some risks and act differently both towards herself and
her class.

Gradually she noticed changes, not only in her own
behaviour and feelings but also in the little Virginia, who
responded well to the sessions with a 'nice parent'. In
time the feeling of frustration and inferiority gave way
to one of acceptance and self-liking. She learnt not to

try so hard, allowed things to happen and was able to accept mistakes and failures as a method of learning. The forgotten child inside was no longer ignored, and responded by allowing a strong, calm, positive feeling to replace the one of insecurity, self-doubt and guilt.

HOW DOES IT WORK?

Mother's almond eyes mix with my wife's ancestral hazel
to give my son green flecks in a painter's eye,
but the troubled look is all his own.

A.K. Ramanujan, Drafts

The basic underlying theory to this procedure is to help childhood memories become resolved, rather than cause limitations in the present. Most people are able to conjure up childhood experiences, creating problems in adulthood by their not being laid to rest.

The 'forgotten children' brought to light differ markedly with each person. Generally they are shy, lonely, frightened and feel blamed and bewildered by what is happening to them. They believe (with justification) that they have no control over their lives and fear that this situation will never end. Many manoeuvres have been tried to extricate themselves from their predicaments, all to no avail as they are powerless to influence the adults or other children causing their plight.

Sometimes an isolated incident may be behind present-day problems, as if the film is 'frozen' in a painful memory and the child involved is unable to receive future knowledge, continuing to live immobilised inside that time capsule of fear, anger or frustration. By communicating with the child, in a similar manner to Virginia, they can be 'freed' and released to join the present.

The attitude towards the child during these exercises is very important. Time and patience are essential, and a caring listening approach will work much better than one of advice and direction. Generally it takes some weeks before a rapport develops and the two way communication can occur between the adult and child. In time the child grows and explores new areas of behaviour, creating positive responses in the adult. It is as if they work as a team, helping the continuous internal conversation to deal with the challenges.

As a rule adults who use this technique gain a great deal of pleasure by doing 'something for themselves'. Understanding the rules of a very important game allows them to put effort and energy towards getting better.

It is often necessary to receive support from a close friend, a counsellor or a therapist. This sharing of the problem, the knowledge that a guiding hand is there, enables hurdles to be overcome which often occur initially. These may be due to disliking the child, being insensitive, trying too hard or not recognising the child's needs by being in too much of a hurry.

Although it may seem a bizarre and difficult technique, in fact it is simple and effective. There is a growth of self-esteem, release from harmful restrictions and an increase in confidence, all of which affect the adult's life. The time spent daily on the exercise allows the child to grow and become absorbed into the adult; being brought from a forgotten past into the present allows such an increase in scope (and coping abilities) that attitudes and behaviour promote expansion and change in a positive direction.

A child's spirit is like a child; you can never catch
it by running after it; you must stand
still and, for love, it will soon itself come back.
Arthur Miller, The Crucible

20
CREATIVE VISUALISATION — THE PROFOUND REALITY OF INTERNAL FANTASY

If one picture is worth a thousand words, internal pictures are worth the value you place on understanding yourself.

Our lives are led on many different levels — actual experiences, thoughts and feelings, ruminations about the past or anticipations about the future. But there is also another world, often completely unknown to us, which continues its activity parallel to our conscious awareness.

This other world is one of pictures and their associated emotions. We become aware of its existence in dreams, daydreams and fantasies. We are much more aware of it in childhood, before shoulds and shouldn'ts push us into adulthood, dimming our pictures and severing communication with them.

In order to understand ourselves or alter our behaviour we can analyse our thoughts and attitudes on any available level — this may involve a variety of doctrines or philosophies, from Primal Scream to Jungian analysis to Zen Buddhism. But one very powerful way of understanding the forces controlling our behaviour is to view (and re-view) our internal world of pictures and feelings, a technique called creative visualisation. This method is both simple and delicate — simple in obtaining the pictures, delicate in ways of utilising them.

HOW DO YOU DO IT?

Imagine being on a boat on the Great Barrier Reef off the north-east coast of Australia. Your sensations and awareness are related to the warmth of the sun, the rocking of the boat, the smell of the salt air and pictures of the sky and sea. This is your immediate world, and your feelings relate to these surroundings.

If you put your head under the water your sensations will be altered to a visual blur, feeling wet and having painful eyes, without improving your experience in any major way. If however you put on a mask and snorkel and then look under the water, a whole new experience awaits you. You discover a completely new world, immediately adjacent to the surface world but inaccessible without the simple procedure of donning a mask and snorkel. This new world is a fantasy world of coloured fish and coral, dappled patterns of sunlight and images that float by, all under completely different regulations from the world above. Your associated emotions alter with your experience, ranging from fear of the unknown to pure delight at the enchantment presented to you.

So it is with creative visualisation. There is a completely different world available using simple techniques of imagination and fantasy. This internal world is populated by mystical beasts, tunnels and caves, waterfalls and lakes, and fantastic journeys such as are described by science fiction. Often the pictures are dramatic, colourful and as real as reality. They contain elements of fear similar to the excitement of a big dipper at a funfair. All are already there and always have been, just as the coral and the undersea life of the Barrier Reef awaited discovery for thousands of years.

Creative visualisation has a multitude of applications.

The one I wish to describe here uses the internal pictures in a non-directive way, allowing them to guide us towards a solution to problems in our 'real life'. This may mean 'looking at' emotions, challenges or difficulties in visual form and allowing ourselves to follow whatever journey is projected. In fact it is more than a projected movie — it is a reality to the person experiencing it, with all the appropriate feelings occurring as well.

 · To use this process requires time, patience, courage to 'face ourselves' and, initially, support from an understanding friend or therapist. It is, as I said, a very simple procedure requiring little other than motivation to change (or to learn more about yourself), the ability to imagine and trust to allow this imagination to take you where it will.

- Have a friend or therapist to support you on your journey.
- Sit quietly for a while, relaxing.
- Be aware you are not to try or necessarily to make logical sense of what happens.
- Focus on some part of your body wherein lies a sensation, such as happiness, headaches, excitement, knots in the stomach, anger, or any other emotion.
- Allow pictures to develop in the site focused upon — let them happen as if you are being led on a journey, and be aware of the associated emotions.
- Have your supporting person guide you without interfering with the process. He/she may ask 'How is that for you?' or 'Would you like to proceed further?' His or her role is to allow you to follow your own images and provide support and care as you do so.

JOURNEYS AND DRAGONS

I fled Him, down the nights and down the days;
I fled Him, down the arches of the years;
I fled Him, down the labyrinthine ways
Of my own mind; and in the mist of tears

I hid from Him, and under running laughter.
Up vistaed hopes I sped;
And shot, precipitated,
Adown Titanic glooms of chasmèd fears,
From those strong Feet that followed, followed after.
The Hound of Heaven, Francis Thompson

Just as one of the threads connecting us to our problems is
the inability to face things, so a common theme of these
visualisations is 'confronting our inner enemies'. And here
a distinct parallel may be drawn with the heroes of Greek
mythology — dragons need to be slayed or Herculean
tasks performed. By facing up to adversity on these
internal journeys, we gain strength, knowledge and
experience to overcome challenges in our personal life.

Thirty-year-old Robert suffered from obsessive
thoughts, which occurred frequently and for no
apparent reason. They limited his enjoyment of life and
caused him fear by 'taking him over' at any time or
place. After a number of consultations we decided to use
visual imagery as a way of understanding how these
panic attacks occurred — 'looking at the problem from
the inside'.

I asked him to relax, close his eyes and focus on how
he felt when the disturbing thoughts occurred. He 'went
into' an area in his chest which he described as 'tense
and pounding', and talked of the experiences that befell
him there. With my help and encouragement the
following story unfolded.

Robert 'It's very dark in here. I feel frightened. It's like
a big cave and I can't get out.'

Brian 'Would you like to put a light on?'

Robert 'Yes. That's better. It's a cave and there's a
tunnel leading to the side.'

Brian 'Would you like to explore the tunnel?'

Robert 'Yes, but I'm a bit nervous. (pause) I'm going
down the tunnel now. It's getting smaller and smaller
and I'm feeling claustrophobic, it's difficult to go on.'

Brian 'Is it OK to go on or would you rather stop?'

Robert 'No. It's OK. I can see some light at the end. I'm squeezing through and it's a lovely lagoon with blue water and a waterfall. I feel great, free and excited. I'm on the lagoon in a boat. I swim up the waterfall. It's a strange feeling of freedom. I know it's illogical but I'm still doing it.' (pause)

Brian 'What's happening now?'

Robert 'I'm floating on a lake, there are lots of islands. I walk up a beach. There is an old man there who beckons me to follow. I'm not sure if I should follow.'

Brian 'What would you like to do?'

Robert 'I think I'll follow. He looks kindly and I have the feeling I should go on but I'm worried how I'm going to get back.' (pause)

Brian 'Are you still with the man on the island?'

Robert 'No. He led me across the island and we jumped off a cliff and started to fly. It was exciting and frightening. We flew above the clouds, higher and higher into outer space. I needed oxygen so put on an oxygen cylinder. You are there too, flying with me, so I give you a cylinder.'

The journey continued, with many challenges and fears, and rewards for facing the difficulties thrust at him by his unseen guide. He gained support by my presence, and allowed the journey to proceed over a number of sessions. He was both in control and not in control at the same time, just as some dreamers can consciously add to their nocturnal dreams. He was able to receive two distinctly different messages at the same time — one that he was in a chair in my consulting room, the other that he was also flying in space.

Over a number of sessions the journey continued, and helped Robert turn down the volume of his obsessive thoughts. We made no direct translation of what they meant, merely allowing them to continue on their own level, in the belief that they were causing changes at other levels.

One conclusion could be that, by facing the mystical and mythical challenges on his fantasy journeys, Robert was able to gain the strength to overcome the obsessive thoughts that had been ruining his life.

I believe this journey was always there for Robert, but he needed support and guidance to enjoy it and strength and courage to put on the 'mask and snorkel' to face it. Once this occurred his undersea world was available to him; his only limits were creativity and ability to overcome the barriers of his own Barrier Reef.

Problems involved with creative visualisation are often related to journeys into the unknown — they are unpredictable and challenging. We never know in advance where we are going or what may appear to test our fears, so it is important to allow time and patience, to go where we need go. Often we need to rest at a safe place along the way and the initial support of a trusted person, just as a mountain climber does.

The beauty of such journeys is that they are free from the fetters of commonsense or analytical understanding. One can move vast distances and make inroads into a difficulty, unhampered by logical thoughts; remarkable results are achieved without even understanding the cause of the problems from a surface point of view.

Often the pictures and journeys are of the Alice in Wonderland variety, adding to the charm and adventure of it all. Generally people do not recount them to others 'in case they think I'm mad' and — if they do, they may well be misunderstood.

Those who experience such journeys are as excited and exhilarated as a child appearing from the funfair river caves, who has explored the dark, overcome his fear, been enchanted by the fantastic sights within and emerged into the sunlight, eyes aglitter from the world he has just encountered.

The path to the magical panorama is through the doorway of feeling.

21
REFLECTIONS ON THE HEALING PROCESS

Every Day in Every Way, I'm getting Better and
Better.

autosuggestive routine, Emile Coué

In the context of this book, 'healing' means getting better,
overcoming difficulties, healthy change or just achieving
peace of mind. Previous chapters have illustrated a great
many factors related to coping with life, so understanding
some of the rules of change will make our passage easier
and more satisfying.

GETTING BETTER IN STAGES

When I first began counselling, I believed that people
improved on a straight line gradient (see the anticipated
graph of change) as they gathered knowledge and insight.
I expected positive change between each visit, with
associated improvement towards an anticipated goal.

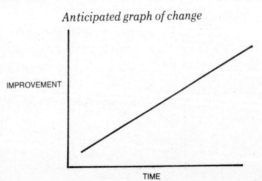

Anticipated graph of change

IMPROVEMENT

TIME

All too often I realised this was not the case. Each peak of 'success' was followed by a trough of 'failure'. Due to the anticipation of a smooth pathway to health, these setbacks caused doubt, concern and an attitude of hopelessness for continued counselling. Time and time again progress was followed by collapse, forward change resulted in backward steps towards the original situation. This was especially so in long-term problems where, over months or years, the symptom had become entangled in every aspect of the person's lifestyle. The more we both expressed dismay at the 'failures', the slower change occurred, and defeat was accepted in the battle for improvement.

By reviewing a great many case histories it became apparent that the graph of change is not a straight line but a spiked one, with gradual upward improvement over a period of time (see the realistic graph of change). Perhaps this step-by-step change occurs due to unconscious fear limiting any rapid improvement. It is as if change needs time for adaption, the process being slowed down to an appropriate rate by the interspersal of setbacks.

Having this knowledge I was then able to forewarn my patients that pitfalls could be expected along the pathway to health — necessary pit-stops, allowing the mind and body to assess progress and the rate of change. The phrase 'Better the devil you know that the one you don't' is perhaps appropriate, explaining the reticence of the unconscious mind to allow major moves from the status

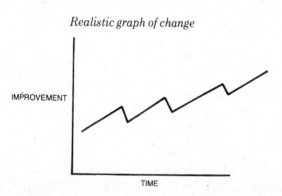

Realistic graph of change

IMPROVEMENT

TIME

quo. And not only is any change going to affect the person concerned, but also others in his surrounding system — family, workmates and social relationships. They too need their own time to adapt to alterations of attitude or behaviour, and will unknowingly put a brake on too rapid progress.

By focusing our attention on what we can learn from the setback, we turn it into a positive event. Learning to accept the fluctuations as part of the process of healing allows us to observe them, rather than adding further problems by being despondent and depressed with their occurrence.

HOW LONG DOES IT TAKE?

If someone sits on a cactus and 100 spines stick into his bottom, he will be in severe pain. By going to his doctor and having a few spines removed each week he will remain in pain until the last one has gone. Sixty painful spines feel very similar to 100; even though great progress has been made towards a pain-free bottom, it is not appreciated by the sufferer.

Having no expectations allows progress to occur without the hindrance of repeated disappointments. And by being involved with the process of change we neither set our sights too high nor compound the problem with dismay and despair. It may well be that the healing process provides us with an opportunity to learn about ourselves; those who achieve the most success have an open, flexible mind, recognising the symptom as only part of the picture.

It is very difficult to predict the time taken for change. Many people naturally ask 'How long before my problem will be solved?' I can only answer, 'It is often difficult to assess the time healing will take. Don't allow time to be your master. Be patient. You have had your condition for months (or years); change may not be as rapid as you wish. Focus your attention on the role you are playing in maintaining the problem, in the progress you have already made rather than the goal you are reaching for. This will give you heart and encouragement to proceed, rather than concern for the hurdles ahead.'

In response to complaints about improvements being too slow, I often ask 'Is it better, worse or the same as it was a few weeks ago?' If it is better — however slightly — there is no need for concern, as you know you are moving in the right direction. If it is worse that before, well, we can learn from the factors which produced this setback. And if there is no change, could it be you need a pause, time to rest, or are there alterations required to overcome the inertia preventing change?

WHAT IS INVOLVED?

Psychological change (change in the mind, attitude, behaviour, balance) differs from the process of removing a diseased organ such as an appendix. If the operation is performed successfully the patient is 'cured' of appendicitis; that is, his disease will not return. But 'cure' is not a word I use when it comes to long-term problems. Life continues, so symptoms are not 'cured, never to return': they are dealt with, overcome, incorporated into a more suitable lifestyle or discarded as being no longer necessary. In the process of understanding the symptom, an increased self-confidence and improved attitude will hopefully prevent its return.

Research has shown that important components of health and longevity are an optimistic attitude, a sense of humour, a partner to share your life with and a pet. Somehow the ownership and companionship of a pet (even a goldfish) provides a vital ingredient for health. Perhaps it is the ability to confide in someone (something) and have one's thoughts listened to, mirrored and understood that is the basis of the healing process. The research also found that one important causative agent of busy executives' heart attacks was not so much the stress and pressure of work, but underlying unresolved hostility in different areas of their lives.

The healing process is a road towards understanding

yourself, learning from life and releasing symptoms that have helped you on the way. This process of learning will guide you up the stepwise slope towards health. It may not be a simple or rapid journey, as often dealing with one problem reveals another and the journey rather than the destination become the focus of attention.

By learning as much as you can about your problem and the resources needed to deal with it, you will become enmeshed in the process of healing and all the benefits that result from that involvement.

IMPORTANT COMPONENTS OF HEALTH AND LONGEVITY ARE AN OPTIMISTIC ATTITUDE, SENSE OF HUMOUR, PARTNER TO SHARE YOUR LIFE WITH, AND A PET....

22
GUIDELINES FOR THE GAME OF LIFE

You have a much better chance of winning the game by knowing the rules and applying them appropriately.

If all else fails, as a last resort follow the instructions.
                    Advice enclosed with new washing machine

It may well seem pretentious to offer advice about life under such an illustrious heading. However, after many years analysing why people come to grief, it became apparent that a few common failings repeated themselves again and again.

One day whilst daydreaming about the variety of ways people lead their lives, I asked myself 'If someone pointed out my mistakes, would I recognise them, accept them or be able to make use of the guidance offered?'

I came to the conclusion that the information received would be stored in the back of my mind, hopefully to blend with past and future experience and tilt the balance in favour of helping me avoid repetitive mistakes. It would be unlikely to help me directly; rather it would be of indirect help, via the circuitous route of absorbing it into my own lifetime of experience.

The following guidelines are offered in the hope that you too will allow them to blend with your beliefs, providing reference points for future learning. The underlying assumption is that, whatever is happening in your life, it is possible for it to be easier, happier or more successful, and perhaps minimal change may achieve this.

- **Awareness**. The first and most important piece of advice is to be aware of yourself. This entails being aware of your feelings, your attitudes and other peoples' reactions. This awareness is the basis of almost all change. In psychological terms this means wresting control from your unconscious so that you become conscious of what is happening.
- **Facing up to problems**. Associated with awareness is an attitude of facing up to any difficulties (internal or external) rather than avoiding them. It is understandable why we avoid the pain of disappointment and failure but by doing so we will be confronted by a similar challenge (in one form or another) again and again until we do eventually face it. Mythology abounds in metaphorical stories concerning the confrontation of the enemy — slaying dragons, fighting the devil, completing dangerous tasks — all of which could be applied to the problems in our lives.
- **Acceptance of ourselves**. Each of us has a dark side (well demonstrated in the *Phantom of the Opera*) which requires facing and acknowledging as part of ourselves; by doing so we lessen its hold on us. By accepting that we have a jealous (angry, greedy, guilty, etc.) side to our nature we are in a much better position to deal with it than by pretending it does not exist.
- **Learning from experience**. Have an attitude of learning from your experiences; in this way they will become useful, even if mistakes or failure occur. By asking yourself 'What can I learn from this?' your world is enlarged producing gain from even the most serious loss.
- **Self-respect**. Respect for yourself is an ingredient often missing from those who have difficulties coping with their lives. All too often low self-esteem is interwoven with annoyance and lack of personal growth. At times it is very important to be assertive, and with a

poor self-image this is almost impossible.

- **Having a goal**. Having an aim and being positive in achieving that aim is a useful framework for short or long-term achievements. Very often people flounder by not asking themselves what they want to achieve. Choosing a small goal and putting effort into achieving it represents a small step in the right direction.

- **Having a balance**. It seems there are two main behaviours we are involved in — doing and being. The first requires effort and an attitude of striving; the second requires acceptance, calmness and inner peace. Having a balance of these two and using each at appropriate times allows the game of life to flow more smoothly and successfully.

- **Discover the real you**. Learning more about yourself and where you are in your life; too many people you to become aware of your needs and any self-restrictions denying them. This self-awareness will point out whether your world is expanding with time. By being comfortable with yourself, you build an internal barometer to external situations.

- **Be responsible for yourself**. Take responsibility for yourself and where you are in your life; too many people blame others for their problems. By taking responsibility you automatically hold the reins and put effort into ensuring you go where you want to go, not wait for someone else to do it for you.

- **Allow yourself time**. Lastly allow time for changes to take place. The process of improvement is step-wise so a suitable length of time is required before progress is noticed. By being aware, you will notice in which direction you are moving. It might be necessary for you to do something different to arrive at the destination of your own choice.

IN CONCLUSION

Often, after struggling to depict what I feel and write it down so others may learn, I come across a piece of

poetry that says it all so elegantly in a few words. At those times I ask myself 'Why write? Why not direct others to read and learn from the poets?'
I have no answer to that question, but wish to illustrate the point with lines from a poem by Thomas Blackburn, commenting on the effects he has had upon his daughter in the poem 'For a Child'.

> and have I put upon your shoulders then,
> what in myself I have refused to bear,
> my own and the confusion of dead men,
> you of all these, my daughter, made my heir.

The poems ends with the lines

> may chaos though have light within your mind,
> and be of use.

I hope that any chaos that exists in your life becomes similarly illuminating, and that any tears you shed will provide the nourishment necessary for your real self to grow.

AUDIO CASSETTES

Recognising the limitations of the written word, audio cassettes have been made to expand and give practical applications of some of the theories discussed in this book. For information, please contact:

Sound in Mind Cassettes
Synergy Centre
1 Cadogan Gardens
London SW3 2RJ
01-730-0720

All Optima books are available at your bookshop or newsagent, or can be ordered from the following address:

Optima, Cash Sales Department,
PO Box 11, Falmouth, Cornwall TR10 9EN

Please send cheque or postal order (no currency), and allow 60p for postage and packing for the first book, plus 25p for the second book and 15p for each additional book ordered up to a maximum of £1.90 in the UK.

Customers in Eire and BFPO please allow 60p for the first book, 25p for the second book plus 15p per copy for the next 7 books, thereafter 9p per book.

Overseas customers please allow £1.25 for postage and packing for the first book and 28p per copy for each additional book.